Richard Morgan

Cambridge IGCSE®

Computer Science

Programming Book

for Microsoft® Visual Basic

CAMBRIDGE
UNIVERSITY PRESS

CAMBRIDGE
UNIVERSITY PRESS

University Printing House, Cambridge CB2 8BS, United Kingdom

Cambridge University Press is part of the University of Cambridge.

It furthers the University's mission by disseminating knowledge in the pursuit of education, learning and research at the highest international levels of excellence.

Information on this title: education.cambridge.org

First published 2015

Printed in the United Kingdom by Latimer Trend

A catalogue record for this publication is available from the British Library

ISBN 978-1-107-51864-3 Paperback

Cambridge University Press has no responsibility for the persistence or accuracy of URLs for external or third-party internet websites referred to in this publication, and does not guarantee that any content on such websites is, or will remain, accurate or appropriate. Information regarding prices, travel timetables, and other factual information given in this work is correct at the time of first printing but Cambridge University Press does not guarantee the accuracy of such information thereafter.

IGCSE® is the registered trademark of Cambridge International Examinations.

....

....

All examination-style questions, sample mark schemes, solutions and/or comments that appear in this book were written by the author. In examination, the way marks would be awarded to answers like these may be different.

Contents

Introduction

When I wrote this book I had two aims in mind. The first was to provide a programming book that specifically covered the material relevant to the Cambridge IGCSE® syllabus. The second, and perhaps more important, aim was to provide the student with a start to the exciting and rewarding process of being able to create their own computer programs.

Language

The syntax and structures used to implement programming techniques will vary across different languages. The book is entirely based around Visual Basic, one of the three recommended languages for the A Level syllabus. Visual Basic offers the student, as a programmer, two modes of application. There is a simple console window in which the student can learn and develop programming skills. It also offers a Windows Forms application, which allows the student to program commercial-style applications that offer a graphical user interface through which users can interact with programs.

The language is supported by a fully functional development environment called Visual Studio Express, which is available free directly from Microsoft. They also provide excellent support and language-specific tutorials via the Microsoft Developer Network. All the code and language specific comments in this book relate to Visual Studio Express 2013.

Examination focussed

The course will test computational thinking independent of any specific programming language. It will do this through the use of program design tools such as structure diagrams and flowcharts. It will also make use of pseudocode, a structured method for describing the logic of computer programs.

It is crucial that the student becomes familiar with these techniques. Throughout this book all the programming techniques are demonstrated in the non-language-specific format required. This will help prepare the student to answer the types of question they will meet in their studies.

To support learning, many of the chapters include examination-style tasks. Chapter 13 has examples of appropriate code solutions showing how to turn logical ideas into actual programs. There is also a series of examination-style questions in Chapter 12, which has a sample mark scheme giving possible solutions and showing where the marks might be awarded.

Developing programming skills

One of the advantages of Visual Basic is that it provides a language that encourages the student to program solutions making use of the basic programming constructs: sequence, selection and iteration. Although the language does have access to many powerful pre-written code libraries, they are not generally used in this book.

Computational thinking is the ability to resolve a problem into its constituent parts and to provide a logical and efficient coded solution. Experience tells me that knowing how to think computationally relies much more on an understanding of the underlying programming concepts than on the ability to learn a few shortcut library routines.

This book is aimed at teaching those underlying skills which can be applied to the languages of the future. It is without doubt that programming languages will develop over the coming years but the ability to think computationally will remain a constant.

How to use this book: a guided tour

Chapter – each chapter begins with a short list of the facts and concepts that are explained in it.

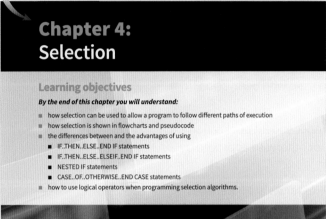

Chapter 4:
Selection

Learning objectives

By the end of this chapter you will understand:

- how selection can be used to allow a program to follow different paths of execution
- how selection is shown in flowcharts and pseudocode
- the differences between and the advantages of using
  - IF..THEN..ELSE..END IF statements
  - IF..THEN..ELSE..ELSEIF..END IF statements
  - NESTED IF statements
  - CASE..OF..OTHERWISE..END CASE statements
- how to use logical operators when programming selection algorithms.

When writing a FOR loop in Visual Basic you need to follow this format:

```
For i = 1 To 10
    'Code to execute
Next
```

Each individual element of the loop performs an important role in achieving the iteration as shown in Table 5.2.

Table 5.2

Element	Description
For	The start of the loop
i = 1 To 10	i is a counter variable that records the number of iterations that have been run. This is usually incremented by 1 every iteration. In Visual Basic there is no requirement to declare the counter variable separately – it is automatically declared as part of the FOR loop. The value of the counter variable can be used within the loop to perform incremental calculations.
Next	The end of the iteration section
	The value of the counter variable is incremented and the flow of the program goes back to the For. The loop will evaluate if the counter value is within the condition (10 in this example). If the counter has exceeded the end value, the loop will direct the flow of the program to the line of code following Next; if not it will rerun the loop.

Any code that is placed within the FOR loop will be repeated on each iteration. The repeated code can itself include complex processes such as selection or additional loops.

KEY TERM

FOR loop: A type of iteration that will repeat a section of code a known number of times.

TIP

As the conditions are checked at For, Next will always pass execution of the loop back to For to check the conditions. It is a common misconception that once the maximum number of iterations has been reached Next will exit the loop. This is not true. Consider a situation where a FOR loop is written to execute 10 times. Although the loop counter may have reached 10 Next will still increment to counter to 11 before passing execution to For. The value of the loop counter will be outside the criteria and For will then exit the loop.

A system is required to output the multiples of a given number up to a maximum of 10 multiples. For example the multiples of 6 are 6, 12, 18, 24, 30, 36, 42, 48, 54 and 60. Figure 5.1 shows the flowchart and pseudocode for the design of the algorithm. Although the counter is automatically declared in Visual Basic this is not the case with all languages so it is normal to include the declaration in the design.

SYLLABUS CHECK

Pseudocode: understand and use pseudocode for counting (e.g. Count ← Count + 1).

Syllabus Check – links programming concepts explained in the text to the Cambridge IGCSE syllabus.

Extension Task – extension of an existing exercise for the student to further develop their knowledge and understanding.

EXTENSION TASK

1 Program a system which takes as inputs:
  - the length of the base of a triangle
  - the perpendicular height of the triangle.

The system will output the area of the triangle.

2 Program a system which takes as inputs:
  - the average speed of a car over the length of a journey
  - the distance that the car has to travel.

The system will output in minutes the length of time the journey will take.

3 Program a system that takes the three inputs required to calculate the area of a trapezoid and outputs the area.

4 Program a system that takes the length of one side of a regular octagon and outputs the resultant area of the octagon.

Summary

- Programs use variables and constants to hold values.
- Variables and constants have identifiers (names) which are used to refer to them in the program.
- Variables are able to have the value they contain changed during the execution of the program. The values within constants cannot be changed while the program is running.
- It is important to select the appropriate data type for the variables and constants. A mismatch between the selected data type and its intended use could result in the program crashing or producing unexpected results.
- Mathematical operators can be used with values held in numeric variables.
- When designing algorithms it is crucial to consider the logical sequence of execution. It is important to declare and initialise appropriate variables as well as obtaining user input before completing any processing.

Summary Checklist – at the end of each chapter to review what the student has learned.

TASK

FOR Loop

1 Extend the multiply system to include two inputs. The first input is the number to multiply, the second is the number of multiples required.

2 Produce a system that accepts two numbers A and B and outputs A^B. For example if A = 3 and B = 4, the output will be 81 ($A^4 = A \times A \times A \times A$).

Task – exercises for the student to test their knowledge and understanding.

Key Term – clear and straightforward explanations of the most important terms in each chapter.

Tip – quick suggestions to remind the student about key facts and highlight important points.

Acknowledgements

The authors and publishers acknowledge the following sources of copyright material and are grateful for the permissions granted.

Cover Soulart/Shutterstock; p. 1 isak55/Shutterstock; p. 13 aimy27feb/Shutterstock; p. 19 Image Source/Getty Images; p. 31 Magictorch/Ikon Images/Getty Images; p. 51 alexaldo/ iStock/Getty Images; p. 67 Ioana Davies (Drutu)/Shutterstock; p. 77 Devrimb/iStock/Getty Images; p. 85 Mclek/Shutterstock; p. 93 Kutay Tanir/Photodisc/Getty Images; p. 103 ILeysen/ Shutterstock; p. 113 Kamil Krawczyk/E+/Getty Images; p. 114 John Howard/Science Photo Library

Screenshots of Microsoft Visual Studio Express 2013 for Windows used with permission from Microsoft.

Cambridge IGCSE® Computer Science Programming Book is an independent publication and is not affiliated with, nor has it been authorized, sponsored, or otherwise approved by Microsoft Corporation.

The publisher has used its best endeavours to ensure that the URLs for external websites referred to in this product are correct and active at the time of going to press. However, the publisher has no responsibility for external websites and can make no guarantee that a site will remain live or that the content is or will remain appropriate.

Chapter 1:
Visual Studio Express

Learning objectives

By the end of this chapter you will understand:

- the two programming applications used in this book
- how to code and save a basic program in Console Application
- how to obtain input data and provide output in Console Application
- how to code and save a basic program in Windows Forms Application
- how to use the main programming windows in Windows Forms Application
- the format of the event-driven subroutines used in a Windows Forms Application.

1.01 Getting Visual Studio Express 2013 for Windows

Visual Studio Express 2013 is the current version of free developer tools provided by Microsoft. They include the programming languages Visual Basic, Visual C++ and Visual C#. The examples in this book have been produced using Visual Studio Express for Windows.

I have used Visual Basic with both GCSE and A Level students for the last five years as it provides an interface that allows students to develop programming skills while at the same time producing satisfying systems. Visual Basic also provides programmers with access to a large class library. Classes are templates that hold prewritten code that support functionality of objects. As students' skills increase they are able to use this feature-rich development environment to produce and publish complex systems. System requirements and download options can be found at www.visualstudio.com/products/visual-studio-express-vs.

1.02 The Integrated Development Environment (IDE)

The default start page for Visual Studio Express 2013 is shown in Figure 1.01. It consists of a number of connected windows which offer different functionality based on the type of project that you open. To begin select New Project.

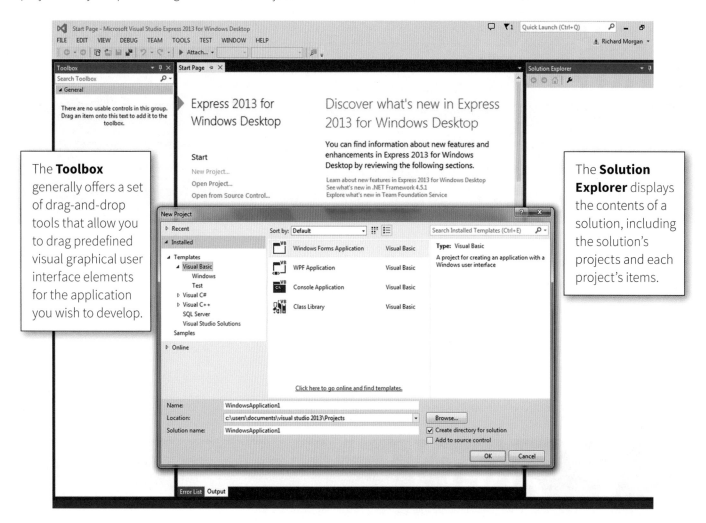

The **Toolbox** generally offers a set of drag-and-drop tools that allow you to drag predefined visual graphical user interface elements for the application you wish to develop.

The **Solution Explorer** displays the contents of a solution, including the solution's projects and each project's items.

Figure 1.01 Visual Studio Express start window

The New Project window provides you with a choice of types of application. The two that are used in this book are Console Applications and Windows Forms Applications. Both make use of very similar coding approaches to algorithms but differ in the way that a user interfaces with them.

A Console Application provides a textual interface uncluttered by the need to support a graphical user interface (GUI). Although IGCSE does not stipulate the use of any programming language or mode the Console Application is the required format in the A Level syllabus.

A Windows Forms Application provides a graphical user interface that can be customised to provide users with visual input, output and processing options. The flow of the program is largely controlled by routines that are triggered in response to the user interacting with the interface.

To create a new project select the preferred application type (in this case, Console Application), change the default name to something meaningful and select OK.

1.03 Console Application

The default layout of the console mode consists of the main **programming window** (see Figure 1.02) which provides an area in which you write the program code required to accept inputs, process data and produce the required outputs. The **Solution Explorer** displays the contents of a solution, which includes the solution's projects and each project's items. This is where you will find the program you have written, listed as a .vb file.

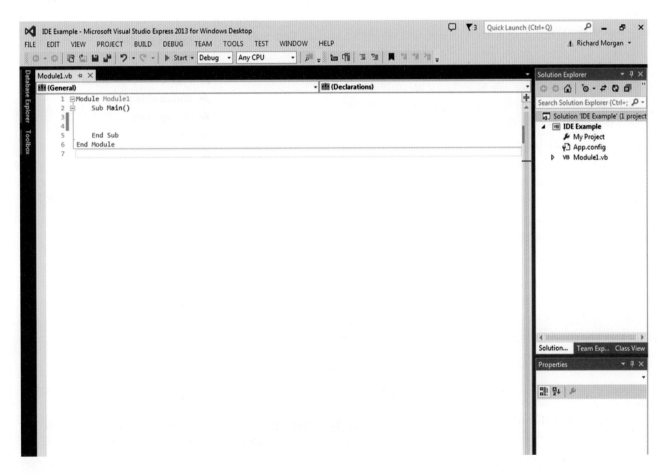

Figure 1.02   Console application programming window

1.04 Make Your First Program using Console Mode

When the console mode is first loaded the code window will contain four lines of code.

```
Module Module1

    Sub Main()
    End Sub

End Module
```

A module is a container of code and can hold a number of subroutines that perform specific actions. `Sub Main()` is the entry point for the program and `End Sub` indicates the end of the subroutine. Code written between these points will be executed when the application is run. You can use the Enter key to add additional lines.

To produce the text 'Hello World' you need to code the application to display the required text.

In Visual Basic the functionality of a class is accessed by use of the dot symbol. Reading inputs and displaying outputs makes use of the Console class which provides access to a library of methods that allow the user to interact with the console.

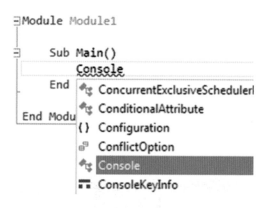

Figure 1.03 Auto-completion window

Type the word 'Console' into the code window (see Figure 1.03). As you type you will notice that the IDE provides an auto-completion window listing all the code inputs or objects that match the letters you have typed. You can double click the correct item, or press Spacebar when the item is highlighted, to auto-complete the entry. This will speed up your coding as once you have typed in the first few characters of the instruction the software will automatically highlight the closest match.

When Console has been completed type a dot symbol. This will show a list of all the available methods for the Console class (see Figure 1.04). The method we need is WriteLine which will display a textual value in the console window when the code is executed. The method has to be passed the required text. To provide the required text the full line will be:

```
Console.WriteLine("Hello World")
```

Figure 1.04 Methods window

Note that the text to be included is in speech marks to indicate that it is text and not a reference to another object. This code will display the required text in a console window when the application is run but the window will close as soon as the code has been executed. To prevent this, the console ReadKey method is used to pause the execution until a key is pressed on the keyboard. The final code will be:

```
Module Module1
    Sub Main()
        Console.WriteLine("Hello World")
        Console.ReadKey()
    End Sub
End Module
```

TIP
Type **Imports System.Console** before the **Module Module1** line to avoid having to type 'Console' every time you need to use the class.

To run the code click the Start option on the toolbar ▶ **Start** ▾ or use F5 from the keyboard. This will launch the console window (Figure 1.05) and display the text 'Hello World'. The execution of the code will be halted until a key is pressed at which time the window will close.

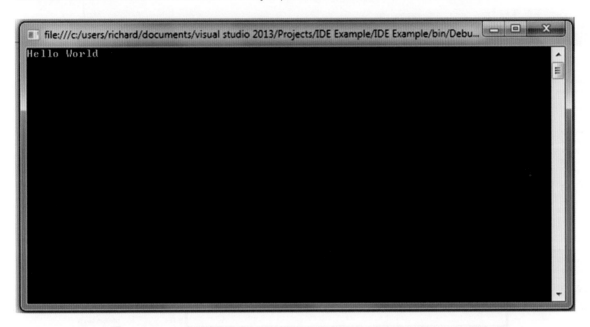

Figure 1.05 Console window

Your first console mode program is complete.

Use 💾 **Save All** or the **Save All** option under the **FILE** menu to save your project.

1.05 Windows Forms Application

Console mode makes use of a single user interface to accept text-based inputs and display text-based outputs. Windows Forms provides a visually richer environment which makes use of a range of graphical user interface tools, to produce systems that have more in common with commercial applications.

The interface is more complex as programmers are required to design and produce the graphic user interface that will allow the user to interface with the system. Visual Basic is an event-driven procedural language in which events trigger subroutines that execute the code within them. In this first Windows Forms application clicking a button on the form will trigger an event that delivers the message 'Hello World'.

The default layout (Figure 1.06) contains five main windows.

Main design and programming window

Solution Explorer

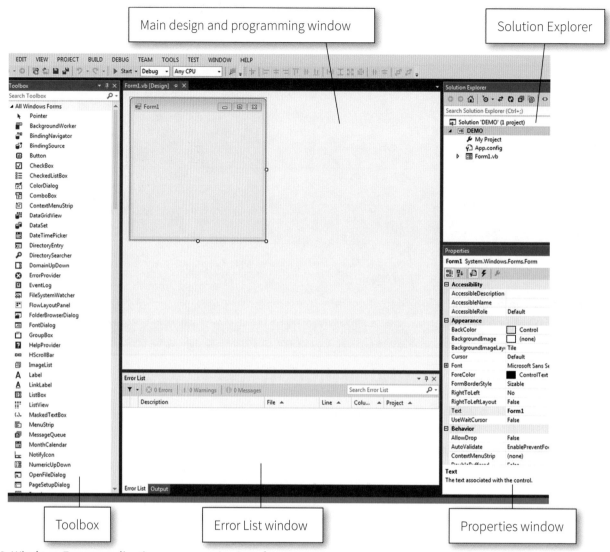

Toolbox

Error List window

Properties window

Figure 1.06 Windows Forms application programming interface

Main design and programming window provides an area in which you design your system's interface and write the program code required to accept inputs, process data and produce the required outputs.

Solution Explorer displays the **contents of a solution**, which includes the solution's projects and each project's items. This is where you will find your forms and the program files that support them.

Toolbox provides a set of tools that will allow you to use predefined visual GUI and control objects for the application you wish to develop.

Properties window is used to view and edit configuration-independent, design-time properties and events of selected objects.

Error List window displays any errors, warnings or messages produced as you edit and compile code.

TIP
Individual windows can be docked or set as floating. It is possible to open windows via the **View** menu, and the **Window** menu.

1.06 Make Your First Windows Forms Application

In a Windows Forms Application the traditional 'Hello World' message will be achieved in two steps:

1   Design and construct the user interface

2   Code the program that will generate the required output.

Design the Interface

Find the button object 🔘   **Button** in the Toolbox. Click to select the tool and move the mouse over the form in the main design window. The mouse icon will change to show the icon of the selected tool. Click and drag will generate a button on the form. Using the standard Windows mouse controls it is possible to resize and move the button.

Use the same process to generate a textbox object 🔲   **TextBox** on the form.

It is considered good practice to give objects meaningful identifiers. An identifier is the name of the object. The default identifier structure is the type of object followed by an increasing number of the objects of that type on the form, such as Button1. The Properties window provides the interface to change the properties of the each object. As you select an object on the form, or the actual body of the form itself the Properties window will change to reflect the properties of the object or form. Objects have many properties that can be configured by the designer but we are initially interested in the properties in Table 1.01.

Table 1.01

Property	What it is
⊟ **Design** 　　(Name)	The identifier (name) used in the code to identify the object
⊞ **Font**　Microsoft Sans 　Text　**Button1**	The font style used to display text on or in the object The text that will appear on the object

Use properties to give the button and the textbox meaningful identifiers.

Code the Program

To create or edit the program code that will be activated by the form you have designed you will need to open the code window.

To open the code window select ‹› **Code** from the **VIEW** menu. The code window will open as an additional tab in the main design window. Clicking the tabs will switch between design and code windows.

It will contain only two lines of code but they are important as they indicate the start and end of the code attached to the form (Figure 1.07). All additional code will be placed between these two indicators. Generally code placed outside will not be part of the form and will cause an error. The Enter key can be used to make additional lines.

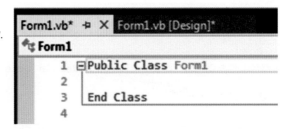

Figure 1.07 Windows Forms application code window

Visual Basic is an event-driven procedural language in which events trigger subroutines that execute the code within them. In this first program clicking the button on the form will trigger an event that delivers the message 'Hello World'. Before writing code the event subroutine has to be created. Creating an event requires you to select the general object and then the specific declaration required. For example, the Button object can have declaration events such as 'click' and 'mouse over'. These different events can be used to trigger different subroutines.

Figure 1.08 shows both of the drop-down menus but it is not possible for you to view both lists simultaneously in the IDE. When you select an object (from the list shown on the left), the list of declarations (shown on the right) shows only the events that are relevant to this object. Click on the Button1 object to select it. The drop-down menu provides a list of all the possible button events. Select 'Click' to insert the Button Click event.

Figure 1.08 Object and Event Declaration selection

TIP

Double clicking an object in the Design window is a shortcut to opening the code window and creating the event subroutine. The software will open the code window and automatically create the default event associated with the object. For example, a Button object's default event is the Click event.

When you select an event the event code will be inserted into your code window.

```
Private Sub Button1 _ Click(sender As Object, e As EventArgs) Handles Button1.Click

End Sub
```

Let us examine the code to identify what each element achieves. Although this makes use of object-oriented language and is outside of the scope of IGCSE, it is useful to have some understanding of how the process works.

Table 1.02

Code element	Description
Private Sub	The start of an individual subroutine. Private means that the subroutine is only accessible by this form.
Button1 _ Click	The name of the subroutine. The automatic default is to name the routine after the object and event that will trigger the subroutine; however it is possible to rename the subroutine.
(sender As Object, e As EventArgs)	The arguments, or data, that are associated with the event. As this is a button click event the arguments are limited – either the button was clicked or it was not. However events associated with mouse activation, for example, will hold data about the location of the mouse on the form and which mouse button was clicked. You should not change or delete any of this data as your subroutine might not work. As you become a more advanced programmer, you will learn how you can manipulate these sections.
Handles Button1. Click	The named events that the subroutine can handle. In this case clicking Button1 will call the subroutine and execute the code it contains. It is possible to have a single subroutine triggered by multiple events.
End Sub	The end of the subroutine. All the code that is to be executed when the subroutine is called is placed between Sub and End Sub.

In Visual Basic the functionality of a class is accessed by use of the dot symbol. In this example Button1 is an object derived from the Button class and one of the functions available is the Click function. The class library's prewritten code is used when an object of the Button class is clicked. You have no need to write the code – it is contained within the class library and is pretested. As you develop your knowledge of Visual Basic you will find that it makes extensive use of class libraries to provide programmers with functionality.

It is now that we can start to write some code. Within the Button Click subroutine, type in the name of your textbox. As you type you will notice that Visual Basic provides an auto-completion window listing all the code inputs or objects that match the letters you have typed (Figure 1.09). You can double click the correct item, or press Spacebar, to auto-complete the entry.

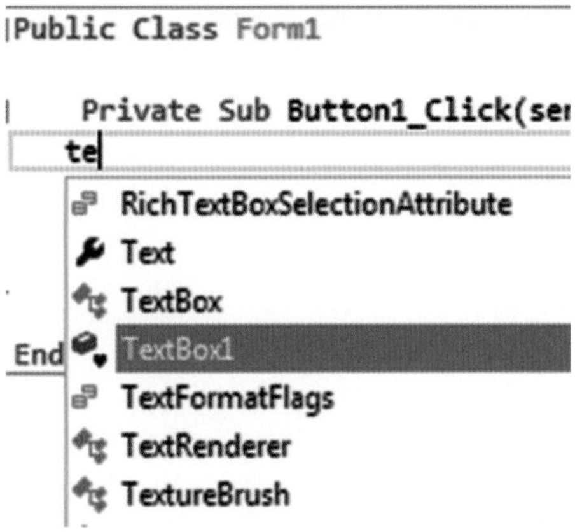

```
Public Class Form1

      Private Sub Button1_Click(ser
      te|
          RichTextBoxSelectionAttribute
          Text
          TextBox
End       TextBox1
          TextFormatFlags
          TextRenderer
          TextureBrush
```

Figure 1.09 Auto-complete window

When the name of the textbox has been entered type a dot symbol. As the textbox is an object of the Textbox class this will show a list of all the available methods which can be attached to a textbox object. The method we need is the Text method which will either set text into a textbox or get text from a textbox (Figure 1.10). Double Click, or press Spacebar, to select this method.

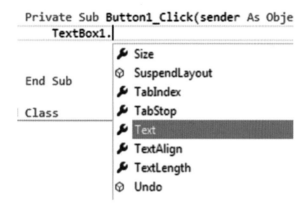

Figure 1.10 List of methods

To indicate the actual text that the method will show in the textbox complete the code as follows:

```
TextBox1.Text = "Hello World"
```

Note that the text to be included is in speech marks to indicate that it is new text and not a reference to another object. The final code will look like this:

```
Public Class Form1

    Private Sub Button1 _ Click(sender As Object, e As EventArgs) Handles Button1.Click

        TextBox1.Text = "Hello World"

    End Sub

End Class
```

To run the code click the Start option on the toolbar ▶ Start ▾ or use F5 from the keyboard. This will launch the form as a separate interactive window. Click on the button and the text 'Hello World' will appear in the textbox.

Your first Windows Forms Application program is complete. You have made use of the design window and the Toolbox to create the interface. You have generated a subroutine called by the Click method of a Button object. Within that subroutine you have used the Text method of a Textbox object to place programmer-defined text into the textbox.

Use 🖫 **Save All** or the **Save All** option under the **FILE** menu to save your project.

1.07 The Code Behind the Form

As you may have expected the interface objects created by the Toolbox are supported by code that draws the objects on the form. This is generated for you (Figure 1.11) as you build the required interface.

```
<Global.Microsoft.VisualBasic.CompilerServices.DesignerGenerated()> _
Partial Class Form1
    Inherits System.Windows.Forms.Form

    'Form overrides dispose to clean up the component list.
    'Required by the Windows Form Designer
    Private components As System.ComponentModel.IContainer

    'NOTE: The following procedure is required by the Windows Form Designer
    'It can be modified using the Windows Form Designer.
    'Do not modify it using the code editor.
    <System.Diagnostics.DebuggerStepThrough()> _
    Private Sub InitializeComponent()
        Me.Button1 = New System.Windows.Forms.Button()
        Me.TextBox1 = New System.Windows.Forms.TextBox()
        Me.SuspendLayout()
        '
        'Button1
        '
        Me.Button1.BackColor = System.Drawing.SystemColors.ButtonFace
        Me.Button1.Location = New System.Drawing.Point(37, 43)
        Me.Button1.Name = "Button1"
        Me.Button1.Size = New System.Drawing.Size(79, 42)
        Me.Button1.TabIndex = 0
        Me.Button1.Text = "Button1"
        Me.Button1.UseVisualStyleBackColor = False
```

Figure 1.11 Example of automatic system generated code supporting the GUI

The file that holds this code is stored in the project folder (Figure 1.12). Until you decide to publish your applications you will not need to have a detailed understanding of the role of the project files.

Name	Type	Size
bin	File folder	
My Project	File folder	
obj	File folder	
Form1.Designer.vb	Visual Basic Source file	3 KB
Form1	.NET Managed Resources File	6 KB
Form1.vb	Visual Basic Source file	1 KB
DEMO	Visual Basic Project file	6 KB
App	XML Configuration File	1 KB

Figure 1.12 Solution Explorer showing project files

1.08 Choosing a Console Application or a Windows Forms Application

Throughout this book the various tasks are completed using one, or sometimes both, of these types of application.

Console Applications offer the benefit of more accurately reflecting the programming style of the IGCSE syllabus and will help prepare you for the expectations of the A level syllabus. In the course, you will not be expected to produce algorithms in any specific language; you will use pseudocode and flowcharts to detail answers to questions. Console applications do not involve the additional complexity of having to reference objects from GUI forms.

Windows Forms Applications will offer a richer visual experience and produce systems similar to those commercially available.

I suggest that making use of both applications will best support the development of your computational thinking.

1.09 Additional Support

The intention of this book is to introduce programming concepts making use of the non-language specific formats included in the syllabus. Visual Basic is used to provide the opportunity for you to use a real programming language to develop your understanding of these concepts. Additional support and guidance on the Visual Basic programming language and Visual Studio Express 2013 can be accessed directly from the Microsoft Virtual Academy.

A range of video tutorials and links to other support can be accessed from
http://www.microsoftvirtualacademy.com/training-courses/vb-fundamentals-for-absolute-beginners

Summary

Visual Studio Express provides two coding windows:

- Console Applications provide a simple interface and are one of the required language formats used in A Level Computing. The interface is a simple text based console through which user inputs and outputs are handled.

- Windows Forms Applications offer a richer visual interface for the user of your programs. They involve the use of a design window and a coding window. They offer more flexibility over the way in which user inputs and outputs are handled.

Chapter 2:
Sequence

Learning objectives

By the end of this chapter you will:

- know the difference between the three programming constructs sequence, selection and iteration
- understand the role of flowcharts and pseudocode when designing programs
- understand the main symbols used in flowcharts
- understand the preferred format of pseudocode.

2.01 Logical Design Considerations

When designing programs it is crucial to consider the order in which the task needs to be completed. All tasks will follow some logical order. When working on a solution to a problem you should first apply the top-down design technique, to break down the big problem into smaller ones.

For example to calculate the time it would take to complete a journey you need to know the distance to be travelled and the intended speed. The first logical step would therefore be to calculate the distance to be travelled as without this data the rest of the task could not be completed.

The **sequence** in which instructions are programmed can be crucial. Consider the following algorithm:

Distance = Speed * Time

Speed = 12 kilometres per hour

Time = 15 minutes

KEY TERM

Sequence: Code is executed in the order it is written.

A human would recognise that the values for speed and time have been given after the calculation. A coded program would simply complete the task in the order given and calculate the distance as zero because at the time of the calculation no values had been provided for speed or time.

A human would probably also recognise the relationship between speed and time, identifying that the speed is quoted 'per hour' but the time is given in minutes and correctly calculate the distance as 3 kilometres (12 * 15/60). Even if the values had been provided before the calculation, as no instructions had been given to convert to a common base the program would calculate distance incorrectly as 180 kilometres by simply multiplying the given values (12 * 15).

2.02 Programming Concepts

Visual Basic and other procedural languages make use of three basic programming constructs. Combining these constructs provides the ability to create code that will follow a logical process. **Selection** and **Iteration** offer a number of alternative approaches and are covered in detail in Chapters 4 and 5.

KEY TERM

Selection: Code branches and follows a different sequence based on conditions being fulfilled.
Iteration: Code repeats a certain sequence a number of times depending on certain conditions.

Sequence

The order in which a process is completed is often crucial to the success of that process. Take the mathematical expression A + B × C + D. The rules of precedence dictate that the multiply operation will be completed first. Had the programmer intended that the operations A + B and C + D be completed before multiplying the two result values then they would have had to be explicit about the required sequence.

In programming the sequence is indicated by the order in which the code is written, usually top to bottom. The program will execute the first line of code before moving to the second and subsequent lines. An example of a sequence error would be completing a process before all the appropriate user inputs had been obtained.

Selection

Often your programs will perform different processes dependent on user input. Consider a system designed to provide access to the school network based on user input of a username and password. The system would need to follow different paths dependent on whether the user input was accurate or not. One path would allow network access if the username and password matched records. If there was no match the system would follow another path in which the user was prompted to re-input details.

Iteration

It is not unusual for a program to perform identical processes on different data items. Consider a program which takes a series of coordinates and produces a line graph. The code that provides the instructions that plot the new coordinates and draw a connecting line from the previous coordinates will be repeated for each of the coordinates given. Iteration provides a method that causes the execution of the code to jump to the beginning of the 'plotting' code sequence for each new set of coordinates.

2.03 Design Tools

When you design programs it is normal to plan the logic of the program before you start to code the solution. This is an important step in the design of effective systems because a flaw in the logic will often result in programs that run but produce unexpected outputs.

The first step in the design process is to break down the problem into smaller problems. This is called 'top-down design'. Once you have the smaller problems defined you can consider each problem separately. This will be easier to plan and finally code. A structure diagram is used to help organise the top-down design. Chapter 6 provides more detail about top-down design and structure diagrams.

The next stage is to design an algorithm for the individual problems. Two approaches that can be used at this stage to help generate logically accurate systems are flowcharts and pseudocode.

To succeed in your course you will be expected to have a working understanding of flowcharts and pseudocode and to be able to use them to answer questions that require you to explain the logic of your solutions to given tasks. Both methods are used throughout this book to indicate the logic of systems and it important that you become familiar with their use.

SYLLABUS CHECK

Problem solving and design: Use flowcharts and pseudocode.

2.04 Flowcharts

Flowcharts are graphical representations of the logic of the intended system. They make use of symbols to represent operations or processes which are joined by lines that indicate the sequence of operations. Table 2.01 details the symbols used.

Table 2.01

Symbol	Use	Example
Terminator	The START or END of a system	START END
Input or output	A required INPUT from the system user or an OUTPUT to the system user The value being input or output is written on the symbol.	INPUT Number OUTPUT Result
Process	A process within the system The flowchart should show sufficient detail to indicate how the proposed process is to be achieved. Beware of making the process too generic. For example if the system was required to calculate an average value, a process entitled 'Calculate Average' would be too generic. It needs to indicate the inputs or other values used to calculate the average.	Result ← A * B Average ← (A+B+C+D)/4
Data flow line	Joins two operations The arrowhead indicates the direction of the flow. Iteration (looping) can be indicated by a flow returning to an earlier process in the flowchart.	INPUT A, B → Result ← A * B → OUTPUT Result
Decision	A point in the sequence where alternative paths can be taken The condition on which the flow is determined is written within the symbol. Where multiple alternatives exist, sequence flows are indicated by chained decision symbols. Each 'No' condition directs to another decision in the process.	YES ← Number above 10 → NO NO → Is Input = A → YES; Is Input = B (NO/YES); Is Input = C (NO/YES)

2.05 Pseudocode

Pseudocode is a method of describing the logic and sequence of a system. It uses keywords and constructs similar to those used in programming languages but without the strict use of syntax required by formal languages. It allows the logic of a system to be defined in a language-independent format for a programmer to code using any programming language which is appropriate to the context.

While the programming code required to perform processes can vary considerable across differing languages, the same pseudocode line could be used to describe the logic of a system intended to be written in any language.

Pseudocode follows a number of underlying principles:

- Use capital letters for keywords close to those used in programming languages.

- Use lowercase letters for natural language descriptions.

- Use indentation to show the start and end of code statements, primarily when using selection and iteration.

One of the advantages of learning to program using Visual Basic is that the actual coding language is structured in a similar way to natural language and therefore closely resembles pseudocode. Visual Basic also automatically indents instructions where appropriate similar to the approach that should be adopted when writing pseudocode.

SYLLABUS CHECK

Pseudocode: understand and use pseudocode for assignment, using ← .

17

2.06 Pseudocode Example

This pseudocode is for an algorithm that accepts the input of two numbers. These values are added together and the result is stored in a memory area called Answer. The value in Answer is then displayed to the user. (In Chapter 3 we will learn that this memory area is known as a variable.)

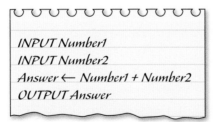

```
INPUT Number1
INPUT Number2
Answer ← Number1 + Number2
OUTPUT Answer
```

Note the use of ← to show the passing of values. This is distinct from the use of the equals symbol (=) which is used to indicate a comparison of two values. (Visual Basic does not have the ← symbol and uses the = symbol in both situations.)

2.07 Effective use of Flowcharts and Pseudocode

Because of the universal nature of flowcharts and pseudocode they are used extensively in the IGCSE Computer Science syllabus.

The aim of this book is to help you to learn to design effective systems using the programming language Visual Basic. The following chapters make use of flowcharts and pseudocode to define the logic of systems, before moving on to specific Visual Basic coded solutions.

Learning how to detail the logic of programs through the use of these design techniques will be a crucial step not only in your preparation for examination but also for your preparation in using the languages of the future. Language syntax is likely to change in the future but the need for effective logical and computational thinking will remain a constant.

Summary

- Programmers make use of three constructs when writing code:
    - sequence: the logical order in which the code is executed
    - selection: branching of code onto different paths based on certain conditions
    - iteration: repeating of sections of code.
- Before coding a program it is crucial to design an appropriate algorithm.
- Flowcharts and pseudocode are tools used in the design of algorithms.

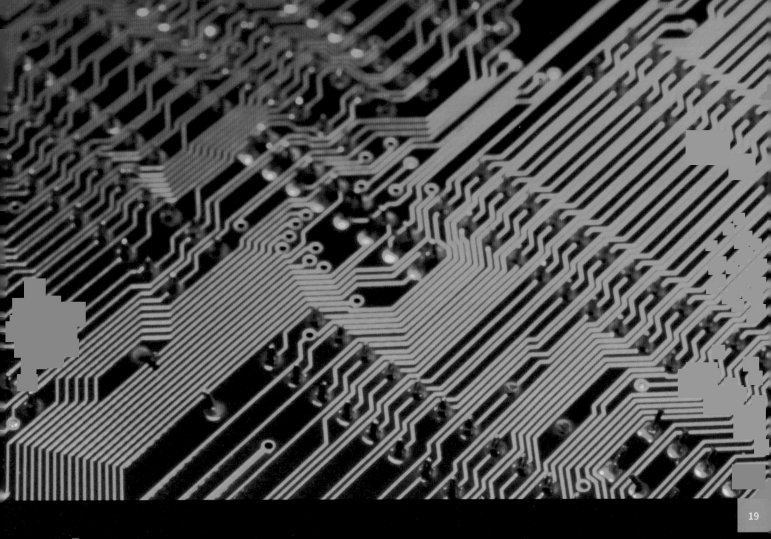

Chapter 3:
Variables and Arithmetic Operators

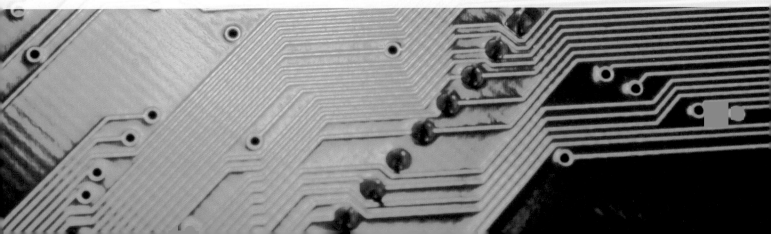

Learning objectives

By the end of this chapter you will understand:

- how to declare and use variables and constants
- and be able to use the data types Integer, Real, Char, String and Boolean
- how to use basic mathematical operators to process input values
- how to design and represent simple programs using flowcharts and pseudocode.

3.01 Variables and Constants

Programs are normally designed to accept input data and process that data to produce the required output. Data used in programs can vary depending on the aim of the program; a calculator will process numerical data while a program designed to check email addresses will process textual data. When writing programs you will use variables or constants to refer to these data values. A **variable** identifies data that can be changed during the execution of a program while a constant is used for data values that remain fixed. The **metadata** you provide about a variable or constant will be used by the computer to allocate a location in memory in which the data will be stored.

KEY TERM

Variable: The identifier (name) given to a memory location used to store data; the value can be changed during program execution.

Metadata: Data about data; information about the structure or format of the data stored.

3.02 Types of Data

In addition to giving the variable or constant an identifier (name) which is used as a label by the computer to reference the allocated memory, it is also important to provide information about the type of data so that the appropriate amount of memory can be reserved. For example storing a large decimal number will require more memory bytes than storing a single character.

To support this process different data types exist. The basic data types you will need to use are identified in Table 3.01.

Table 3.01

Data type	Description and use	Visual Basic
Integer	Whole numbers, either positive or negative Used with quantities such as the number of students at a school – you cannot have half a student.	Can store values ranging from –2 147 483 648 to 2 147 483 647. Uses 4 bytes of memory. If a decimal value is put into an Integer variable, the value is rounded to the nearest whole number.
Real	Positive or negative fractional values Used with numerical values that require decimal parts, such as currency. Real is the data type used by many programming languages and is also referenced in the IGCSE Computing syllabus.	Visual Basic does not use the term Real, the equivalent data type is called '**Decimal**'. The range of values depends on the number of decimal places required. Uses 16 bytes of memory. Stores a much larger range of numbers than the Integer data type. Single and Double also hold fractional numbers.
Char	A single character or symbol (for example, A, z, $, 6) A Char variable that holds a digit, cannot be used in calculations.	Stores a single Unicode character. Uses 2 bytes of memory.
String	More than one character (a string of characters) Used to hold words, names or sentences.	Can store a maximum of approximately 2 billion Unicode characters.

Data type	Description and use	Visual Basic
Boolean	One of two values, either TRUE or FALSE Used to indicate the result of a condition for example, in a computer game a Boolean might be used to indicate if a player has achieved a higher level.	

You can find more information about the data types in Visual Basic at http://msdn.microsoft.com/en-us/library/47zceaw7.aspx.

> **SYLLABUS CHECK**
>
> **Programming concepts:** understand and use Integer, Real, Char, String and Boolean.

3.03 Pseudo Numbers

Telephone numbers and ISBN numbers both consist of digits but are not truly numbers. They are only a collection of digits used to uniquely identify an item; sometimes they contain spaces or start with a zero, and they are not intended to be used in calculations. These are known as 'pseudo numbers' and it is normal to store them in a String data type. If you store a mobile phone number, as an Integer any leading zeros will be removed and no spaces or symbols will be permitted.

3.04 Declaring Variables and Constants

You will need to select an identifier (name) and a data type for your variables or constants. In Visual Basic it is possible to declare variables without declaring a data type but it is considered good practice to define the data type. This is known as 'strong typing'; it allows the compiler to check for data type mismatches and results in faster execution of the code.

> **SYLLABUS CHECK**
>
> **Programming concepts:** declare and use variables and constants.

When naming your variables or constants use identifiers that have a meaningful link with the data being stored. For example if you are storing the high score of two players in a game use the names *Player1HighScore* and *Player2HighScore*. Declaring variables with relevant identifiers will help to make your code easier to read and maintain.

It is not possible in Visual Basic to have spaces in identifiers. For identifiers that incorporate more than one word it is normal to start each new word with a capital letter. This is known as CamelCase. Identifiers can include digits, for example Number1, but cannot begin with a digit. Words that are used by Visual Basic are known as reserved words and cannot be used as variable names. For example it is not possible to name a variable 'Integer' or 'Boolean'.

It is important to select the most appropriate data type for your variables. Using inappropriate data types may result in your programs returning unexpected results. For example using the data type Integer to store currency values could result in the decimal element being rounded and the wrong values being output.

It is also considered good practice to give variables an initial value when declaring them: this is known as 'initialising'. Uninitialised variables will hold the default values set by Visual Basic. Some examinations may expect you to initialise variables so getting into the habit is a good idea.

21

3.05 Declaring Variables in Visual Basic

Declaration of variables is achieved by using the code format shown in Figure 3.01.

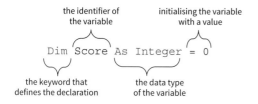

Figure 3.01 Declaring variables in Visual Basic

In the following declarations the variable identifier, data type and initial value are declared.

```
Dim PlayerName As String = ""
Dim DrivingLicence As Boolean = False
Dim Payment As Decimal = 0
```

3.06 Declaring Constants in Visual Basic

The code for declaring constants follows a similar format to that used for variables, but uses the keyword 'Const' to replace 'Dim'.

Here is an example of declaring a **constant**:

```
Const Pi As Decimal = 3.14159
```

KEY TERM

Constant: A named memory location which contains data that can be read but not changed by the program.

3.07 Variable Scope

When declaring a variable the placement of the declaration in the code will determine which elements of the program are able to make use of the variable.

Global variables are those that can be accessed from any routine within the program. They are used for variables that need to be accessed from many elements of your program. To give a variable global status it must be declared outside of any specific subroutine. It is good practice to make all the global declarations at the start of the code.

Local variables can only be accessed in the code element in which they are declared. They are used when the use of the variables will be limited to a single routine. Using local variables reduces the possibility of accidently changing variable values from other code elements.

22

Figure 3.02 shows the same code in a Console Application and in a Windows Forms Application. There are two global variables (Score and PlayerName) and one local variable (Result).

```
Module Module1                        Public Class Form1

    Dim Score As Integer = 0              Dim Score As Integer = 0
    Dim PlayerName As String = ""         Dim PlayerName As String = ""

    Sub Main()                            Private Sub Button1_Click(sender As Object, e As EventArgs)
        Dim Result As Integer = 0                   Handles Button1.Click

    End Sub                                    Dim Result As Integer = 0

End Module                                End Sub
                                      End Class
```

Console mode example | Windows Form mode example

Figure 3.02 Declaring Global and Local Variables

3.08 Arithmetic Operators

There are a number of operations that can be performed on numerical data. Combining these operations and appropriate variables allows you to create programs that are capable of performing numerical computation tasks.

The basic operators used in Visual Basic are shown in Table 3.02.

Table 3.02

Operation	Example of use	Description
Addition	Result = Number1 + Number2	Adds the values held in the variables Number1 and Number2 and stores the result in the variable Result.
Subtraction	Result = Number1 - Number2	Subtracts the value held in variable Number2 from the value in Variable Number1 and stores the result in the variable Result.
Multiplication	Result = Number1 * Number2	Multiplies the values held in variables Number1 and Number2 and stores the result in the variable Result.
Division	Result = Number1 / Number2	Divides the value in variable Number1 by the value in Number2 and stores the result in the variable Result

TIP

As a division operation can result in a fractional value it would be normal to use a Decimal (or Real) data type to hold the Result.

3.09 Programming Tasks

Multiply Machine

The Multiply Machine takes two numbers input by the user, multiplies them together and outputs the resultant value.

First you need to design the algorithm. Figure 3.03 shows flowchart and pseudocode solutions for the task.

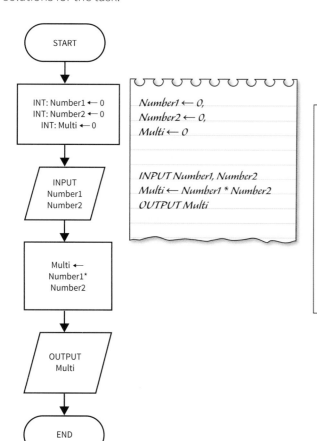

Note the use of the correct and recognised symbols in the flowchart and pseudocode:

- [ ] indicates a process such as completing the multiplication.

- /   / indicates either an INPUT or OUTPUT.

- ← indicates the assigning of a value; it is used when initialising variables or passing new values to a variable.

Figure 3.03 Pseudocode and flowchart for Multiplication algorithm

In Visual Basic assigning is indicated by the use of the = symbol. In pseudocode the ← symbol is used.

TIP

Variables that have been declared with numerical data types such as Integer or Decimal can only accept numerical data.

If textual data is input the software will cause an exception error:

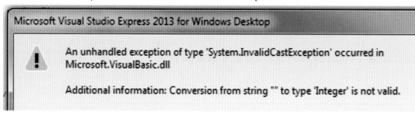

A null input will also cause this error.

Here is the console mode program implementation of this solution:

```
Module Module1

    Sub Main()
        'Declaration and initialising of required local variables
        Dim Number1 As Integer = 0
        Dim Number2 As Integer = 0
        Dim Multi As Integer = 0

        'Display a request for the first number
        Console.WriteLine("Please insert first number")
        'Store the user input into the Number1 variable
        Number1 = Console.ReadLine()

        'Request and store second user input
        Console.WriteLine("Please insert second number")
        Number2 = Console.ReadLine()

        'Storing in the local variable the multiplication result
        Multi = Number1 * Number2

        Console.WriteLine("The answer is")
        'Displaying the value held in the variable Multi
        Console.WriteLine(Multi)

        'ReadKey used to pause the console window
        Console.ReadKey()
    End Sub

End Module
```

If you are using the Windows Forms application you will need to design an interface that is capable of taking two values and displaying a result. It could look something like Figure 3.04.

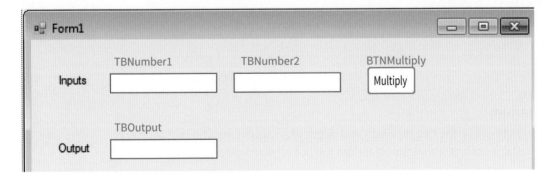

Figure 3.04 Windows Forms interface design

Remember to give the design elements of the form appropriate names. This example has used the names shown in green on Figure 3.04.

25

The code to achieve this solution should be run under the button click event.

```
Public Class Form1

    Private Sub BTNMultiply _ Click(sender As Object, e As EventArgs) Handles BTNMultiply.Click

        'Declaration and initialising of required local variables
        Dim Number1 As Integer = 0
        Dim Number2 As Integer = 0
        Dim Multi As Integer = 0

        'Storing the values input in the textboxes to the variables
        Number1 = TBNumber1.Text
        Number2 = TBNumber2.Text

        'Storing in the local variable the multiplication result
        Multi = Number1 * Number2

        'Displaying the value held in the variable Multi in the output text box
        TBOutput.Text = Multi

    End Sub

End Class
```

Multiply Machine Extension Task

Extend this program to include addition, subtraction and division buttons. It will have to be programmed using a Windows Forms application.

Points for discussion:

1   Should all the variables be declared locally?

2   Is Integer an appropriate data type for all the resultant output variables?

Volume of Water in Aquarium

Design a program where the inputs will be the height, width and depth of an aquarium. The output should be the number of litres of water that the aquarium will hold (1 litre = 1000 cm^3).

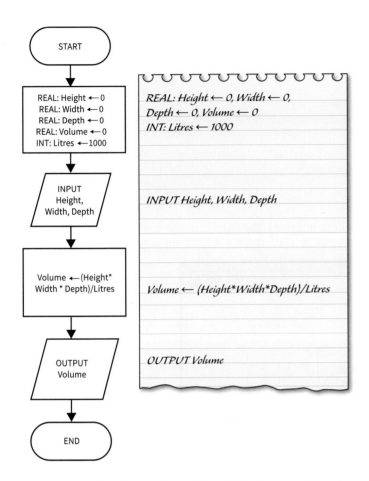

Figure 3.05 Flowchart and pseudocode for the aquarium algorithm

The following code shows the console mode program implementing this solution. Note how the logical sequence of the code follows the flowchart or pseudocode design.

```
Module Module1

    'Global variables to hold the inputs
    'Note the addition of the 1 to the names to overcome the reserved word conflict
    Dim Height1 As Decimal = 0
    Dim Width1 As Decimal = 0
    Dim Depth1 As Decimal = 0
    'Constant to hold the ratio of cubic centimetres to litres
    Const Litres As Integer = 1000

    Sub Main()
        'Local variable to hold the resultant volume
        Dim Volume As Decimal = 0

        'Request and store user inputs
        Console.WriteLine("Please insert Height and press Return")
        Height1 = Console.ReadLine
        Console.WriteLine("Please insert Width and press Return")
        Width1 = Console.ReadLine
        Console.WriteLine("Please insert Depth and press Return")
        Depth1 = Console.ReadLine
```

```
        'Calculate Volume and store in local variable
        Volume = Height1 * Width1 * Depth1
        'Convert the value in volume current in cubic centimetres to litres
        Volume = Volume / Litres

        'Display the value held in the variable Volume
        Console.WriteLine("The volume is")
        Console.WriteLine(Volume)

        Console.ReadKey()
    End Sub
End Module
```

Using the Windows Form application the interface could look something like Figure 3.06.

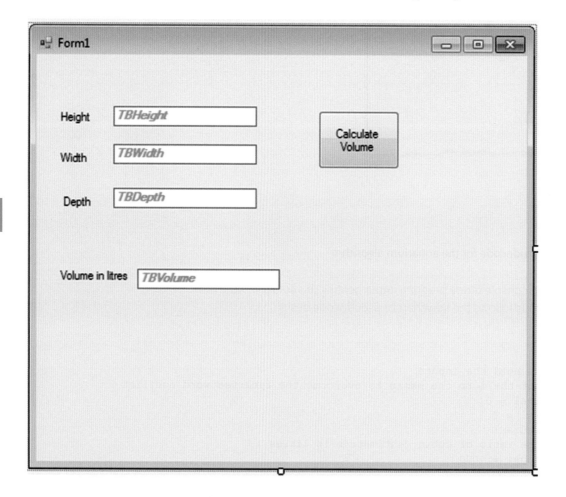

Figure 3.06 Interface design for Windows Forms Aquarium algorithm

Remember to give the design elements of the form appropriate names. Figure 3.06 shows the names in green.

The Windows Form application code to achieve this solution should be run under the button click event:

```
Public Class Form1

    'Global variables to hold the inputs
    'Note the addition of the 1 to the names to overcome the restricted word conflict
    Dim Height1 As Decimal = 0
    Dim Width1 As Decimal = 0
    Dim Depth1 As Decimal = 0
    'Constant to hold the ratio of cubic centimetres to litres
    Const Litres As Integer = 1000

    Private Sub BTNVolume _ Click(sender As Object, e As EventArgs) Handles BTNVolume.Click

        'Local variable to hold the resultant volume
        Dim Volume As Decimal = 0

        'placing values from the textbox into variables.
        Height1 = TBHeight.Text
        Width1 = TBWidth.Text
        Depth1 = TBDepth.Text

        'Calculate Volume and store in local variable
        Volume = Height1 * Width1 * Depth1
        'Convert the value in volume current in cubic centimetres to litres
        Volume = Volume / Litres

        'Output the value in local variable to the textbox
        TBVolume.Text = Volume

        'The volume calculation could have been achieved in one calculation
        'Volume = (Height1 * Width1 * Depth1)/Litres

    End Sub
End Class
```

TASK

Area and Circumference of a Circle

A system takes the radius of a circle as its input and calculates the area of the circle and the circumference.

1 Draw a flowchart and create a pseudocode algorithm that will output the area of the circle and the circumference based on the input radius.

2 Test that your algorithm works by programming and running the code in Visual Basic.

3.10 Development Challenges

Challenge yourself, or your colleagues, to complete a programming task. The following are some examples of the type of task you might like to consider. The last two are complex mathematical challenges.

For each challenge, you should draw a flowchart and create a pseudocode algorithm before programming and running the code in Visual Basic.

EXTENSION TASK

1   Program a system which takes as inputs:

   - the length of the base of a triangle

   - the perpendicular height of the triangle.

The system will output the area of the triangle.

2   Program a system which takes as inputs:

   - the average speed of a car over the length of a journey

   - the distance that the car has to travel.

The system will output in minutes the length of time the journey will take.

3   Program a system that takes the three inputs required to calculate the area of a trapezoid and outputs the area.

4   Program a system that takes the length of one side of a regular octagon and outputs the resultant area of the octagon.

Summary

- Programs use variables and constants to hold values.

- Variables and constants have identifiers (names) which are used to refer to them in the program.

- Variables are able to have the value they contain changed during the execution of the program. The values within constants cannot be changed while the program is running.

- It is important to select the appropriate data type for the variables and constants. A mismatch between the selected data type and its intended use could result in the program crashing or producing unexpected results.

- Mathematical operators can be used with values held in numeric variables.

- When designing algorithms it is crucial to consider the logical sequence of execution. It is important to declare and initialise appropriate variables as well as obtaining user input before completing any processing.

Chapter 4:
Selection

Learning objectives

By the end of this chapter you will understand:

- how selection can be used to allow a program to follow different paths of execution
- how selection is shown in flowcharts and pseudocode
- the differences between and the advantages of using
  - IF..THEN..ELSE..END IF statements
  - IF..THEN..ELSE..ELSEIF..END IF statements
  - NESTED IF statements
  - CASE..OF..OTHERWISE..END CASE statements
- how to use logical operators when programming selection algorithms.

4.01 The Need for Selection

Systems often need to be programmed to complete different processes depending on the input received. For example an automatic door will open if it detects that someone wishes to enter and shut when no presence is detected. Expert systems will provide answers or conclusions based on the user response to previous questions. Both these systems appear to be able to make decisions based on input but the reality is that the system has been logically designed to complete a certain process based on expected input.

In Visual Basic, and many other languages, this is achieved by use of programming techniques known as IF statements or CASE statements. Both techniques perform a similar role with CASE statements generally being considered more appropriate for situations where multiple inputs need to be considered.

4.02 IF Statements

If the process for an automatic door was written down it might appear as 'If a presence is detected then open the door otherwise close it'. In simple terms this is the approach to coding an IF statement. The code provides a condition to evaluate ('if a presence is detected'); the outcome of the condition is either True or False. The code then provides actions depending on the outcome of the condition (if it is True 'open the door'; if it is False 'close the door').

SYLLABUS CHECK

Pseudocode: understand and use pseudocode, using IF..THEN..ELSE..ENDIF.

32

In a flowchart the symbol used to indicate a decision is a diamond. The diamond contains information about the criteria and normally has two exit routes indicating the True and False paths.

The flowchart in Figure 4.01(a) includes the Decision symbol. The TRUE and FALSE paths have been indicated. (When programmed this will become an IF or a CASE statement.) Once the appropriate action has been performed the program flow returns back to 'Check for Presence' and the input is again evaluated by the IF statement.

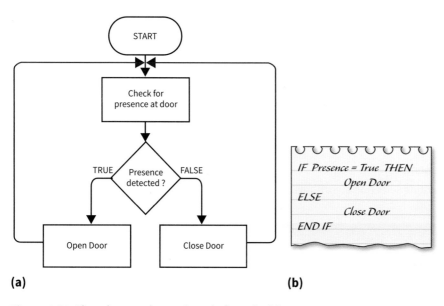

(a) **(b)**

Figure 4.01 Flowchart and pseudocode for a decision

Note that TRUE/FALSE can also be written as YES/NO.

The pseudocode **IF statement** for the flowchart in Figure 4.01(a) is shown in Figure 4.01(b).

The start of the statement is indicated by IF. The condition is written between IF and THEN. The action to be taken if the condition is true follows THEN. The action is indented to improve readability. ELSE indicates any alternative action. Again the action to be taken should be indented. END IF indicates the end of the statement

Not all IF statements have an alternative action and therefore the ELSE may be omitted. This would be appropriate in a situation where the decision results in only one action. For example a system used to calculate the cost of a train fare could apply a discount if the passenger is a child. The system would first calculate the normal fare and then apply the discount if the ticket is for a child. No additional action would be taken if the ticket was for an adult. This pseudocode is for that algorithm:

Calculate TicketPrice
IF Ticket for Child THEN
 TicketPrice ← TicketPrice * Discount
END IF
OUTPUT TicketPrice

KEY TERM

IF statement: A statement which allows the program to follow or ignore a sequence of code depending on the data being processed.

4.03 Logical Operators

In the automatic door example the only possible inputs were 'detected' or 'not detected'. However, many systems depend on less discrete criteria. An air-conditioning system will receive continuous temperature data and will perform actions based on that temperature data. A system for determining examination grades will calculate the grade output by identifying if the students' marks fall within certain grade boundaries.

To support needs of this type, a number of logical operators exist. They tend to follow the accepted mathematical use of the operator symbols. The basic operators supported by Visual Basic are shown in Table 4.01.

Table 4.01

Operator	Description
=	is equal to
>	is greater than
<	is less than
>=	is greater than or equal to
<=	is less than or equal to
<>	is not equal to

The choice of the correct logical operator is important. Using the wrong operator can produce unexpected results in your algorithms. Often the way in which the decision to be made is worded will indicate the appropriate operator to use.

Table 4.02

Decision in words	Appropriate operator	Common errors
Apply a discount for students aged under 16	IF Student < 16 THEN	• Using >: IF Student > 16 would apply the discount for students over 16. • Using <=: IF Student <= 16 would also apply the discount for students aged 16. The wording states UNDER.
Turn on the cooler when the temperature is 10 °C or more	IF Temp >= 10 THEN	• Using =: IF Temp = 10 means the cooler will only operate when the temperature is exactly 10°C. If the temperature rises above 10°C the condition would no longer be true and the cooler would stop. • Using >: IF Temp > 10 means the cooler would not turn on at 10°C as required.

Chapter 9 shows techniques to identify these types of logical error.

4.04 Coding IF Statements in Visual Basic

The code for an IF statement in Visual Basic is very similar to the pseudocode version. Remember one of the advantages of using Visual Basic is the similarity between the actual programming code and pseudocode which helps prepare you for the exam.

```
If Age <= 16 Then
    'Code if condition is true
Else
    'Code if condition is false
End If
```

When typing the statement the IDE software will automatically apply the `End If` once you complete `Then` and press the Return key. Should an `Else` be required you will need to type this. The IDE will automatically indent all the code within the statements.

Figure 4.02 shows a flowchart and the pseudocode for a system that will take as input two whole numbers. If the second number is larger than the first the system will output 'SECOND' if not the output is 'FIRST'.

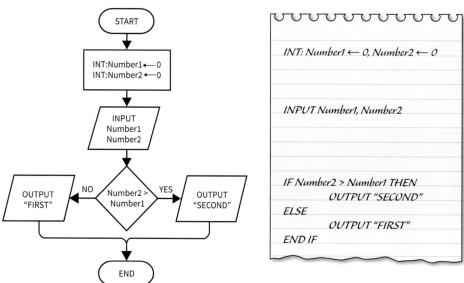

Figure 4.02 Flowchart and pseudocode showing decision

This code implements the system from the flowchart and pseudocode:

```
Module Module1
    Sub Main()
        Dim Number1 As Integer = 0
        Dim Number2 As Integer = 0

        Console.WriteLine("Enter First Number")
        Number1 = Console.ReadLine
        Console.WriteLine("Enter Second Number")
        Number2 = Console.ReadLine

        If Number2 > Number1 Then
            Console.WriteLine("SECOND")
        Else
            Console.WriteLine("FIRST")
        End If

    End Sub
End Module
```

Discussion Questions

TASK

1   Would the same output be achieved by reversing the condition to `Number1 < Number2`?

2   We reword the question to read: *If the second number is* **the same as or larger** *than the first the system will output 'SECOND' if not the output is 'FIRST'. Consider these questions:*
   - How would this impact on the choice of logical operator?
   - Could the condition still be reversed?

4.05 Multiple IF Statements

If the previous example is extended to provide a third output when the numbers are the same, a simple IF statement would be insufficient to solve the problem.

A system will take as input two whole numbers. The system will output:

- SECOND if the second number is larger than the first

- FIRST if the second number is smaller than the first

- SAME if the two numbers are equal.

Now we have three decisions to make, how can this be achieved?

Problems of this nature can be solved by a series of sequential IF statements each of which ends before the following statement starts (see Figure 4.03).

```
Module Module1
    Sub Main()
        Dim Number1 As Integer = 0
        Dim Number2 As Integer = 0

        Console.WriteLine("Enter First Number")
        Number1 = Console.ReadLine
        Console.WriteLine("Enter Second Number"
        Number2 = Console.ReadLine

        If Number2 = Number1 Then
            Console.WriteLine("SAME")
        End If

        If Number2 > Number1 Then
            Console.WriteLine("SECOND")
        End If

        If Number2 < Number1 Then
            Console.WriteLine("FIRST")
        End If

    End Sub
End Module
```

```
INT: Number1 ← 0, Number2 ← 0

INPUT Number1, Number2

IF Number2 = Number1 THEN
OUPUT "SAME"
END IF

IF Number2 > Number1 THEN
OUTPUT "SECOND"
END IF

IF Number2 < Number1 THEN
OUTPUT "FIRST"
END IF
```

Figure 4.03 Sequential IF statement example

Although this approach achieves the required outcome it is inefficient. Consider the situation where both numbers are equal. The first IF statement would have provided the appropriate output and the conditions in the following IF statements are false but the code must still execute the remaining IF statements. The algorithm produces the required output but two IF statements have been executed unnecessarily.

4.06 Nested IF Statements

To avoid the inefficiency of multiple IF statements it is possible to place one or more IF statements entirely within another. The second and subsequent IF statements will only be executed should the first condition prove to be false. These are known as 'nested IF' statements.

The following shows how a Nested IF approach could be applied to the inefficient sequence of IF statements shown in Figure 4.03. Because the second IF statement will only execute if the criteria in the first statement is False unnecessary execution of IF statements is avoided.

- In the flowchart in Figure 4.04 this is indicated by the second decision diamond flowing from the NO output of the first. The YES output of the first decision diamond goes direct to END after the output.

- In the pseudocode in Figure 4.04, the second IF statement (marked in blue) is placed entirely within the ELSE of the first.

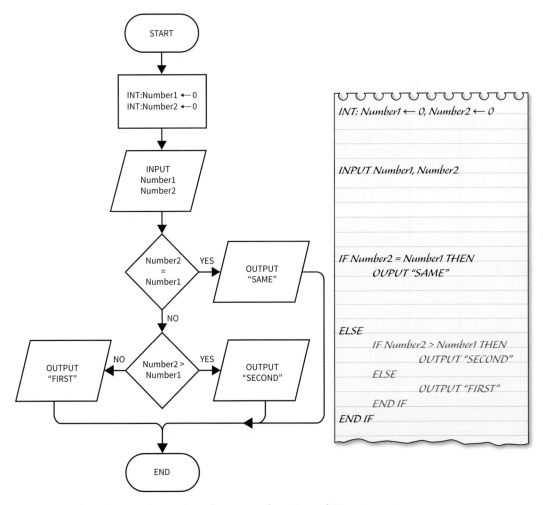

Figure 4.04 Flowchart and pseudocode approach to Nested IF statements

The coded solution would follow the pseudocode, with the second IF statement being NESTED within the ELSE of the first. Notice how the indentation improves readability.

```
If Number2 = Number1 Then
      Console.WriteLine("SAME")
Else
      If Number2 > Number1 Then
          Console.WriteLine("SECOND")
      Else
          Console.WriteLine("FIRST")
      End If
End If
```

SYLLABUS CHECK

Pseudocode: understand and use pseudocode, using CASE..OF..OTHERWISE..ENDCASE.

4.07 CASE Statements

CASE statements are considered an efficient alternative to multiple IF statements. In a CASE statement selection is based on one variable with multiple possible values. It is not possible to generate a CASE statement for multiple variables or conditions that use logical connectors. CASE statements allow complex situations, based on a single variable, to be programmed more easily than using multiple IF statements.

Consider the situation where a user must input one of A, B or C. The code is required to follow different paths depending on which letter has been input. The pseudocode in Figure 4.05(a) shows the approach that would be taken using a combination of IF statements and Figure 4.05(b) shows a CASE statement.

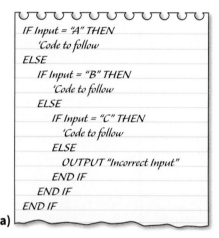

(a)

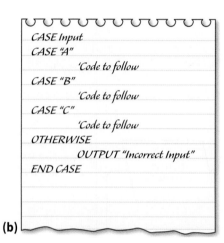

(b)

Figure 4.05 Nested IF and CASE statements

Both approaches achieve the same outcome but the CASE statement is simpler to code and easier to read than the NESTED IF.

KEY TERM

CASE statement: A statement which allows one of several sequences of code to be executed depending on the data being processed.

The two main approaches to flowcharting CASE statements are shown in Figure 4.06.

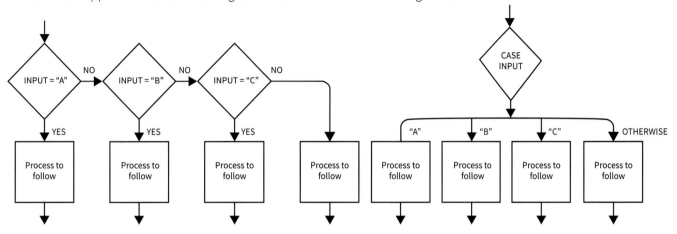

Figure 4.06(a) Flowchart for CASE using sequential decisions   Figure 4.06(b) Flowchart for CASE with multiple branches

Figure 4.06(a) shows the preferred approach in IGCSE. A sequence of connected decisions to show the logical process. This is the same flow chart that would show the NESTED IF approach.

Figure 4.06(b) shows an alternative approach used by some people. A specific CASE symbol leads to multiple decision branches including the OTHERWISE branch.

4.08 Coding CASE Statements in Visual Basic

Programming a CASE statement closely follows the pseudocode. However Visual Basic uses specific keywords which differ from those traditionally used in pseudocode.

```
Select Case Input
     Case Is = "A"
          'code to follow
     Case Is = "B"
          'code to follow
     Case Is = "C"
          'code to follow
     Case Else
          Console.WriteLine("Incorrect Input")
End Select
```

The CASE statement has four main elements discussed in Table 4.03.

Table 4.03

Element	Description
`Select Case Input`	The start of a CASE statement
	The identifier (name) of the variable on which the selection is to be based follows the Case keyword.
`Case Is = "A"` `'code to follow`	A series of statements identifying the values on which the decision is based
	The code path to be followed if the condition is true is indented after the statement.
`Case Else`	The path that is to be followed if all previous conditions are False.
	Similar to the ELSE in an IF statement, this clause does not have to be included in a CASE statement.
`End Select`	The end of the CASE statement

4.09 Programming Tasks

The following example tasks show a NESTED IF and a CASE approach for each situation.

Calculator

In Chapter 3 we created a basic calculator that was capable of taking two numbers and could perform basic arithmetic functions on those numbers depending on which button the user pressed. A real calculator does not work in this way. Instead the first number is input, the arithmetic operator is selected, the second number is input and the answer is obtained by pressing the 'equals' button.

The task is to create a calculator that works in this way:

1   User inputs a number.

2   User selects one of four arithmetic operators.

3   User inputs second number.

4   The appropriate output is provided.

Figure 4.07 shows the flowchart for this task and Figure 4.08 shows the two pseudocode options.

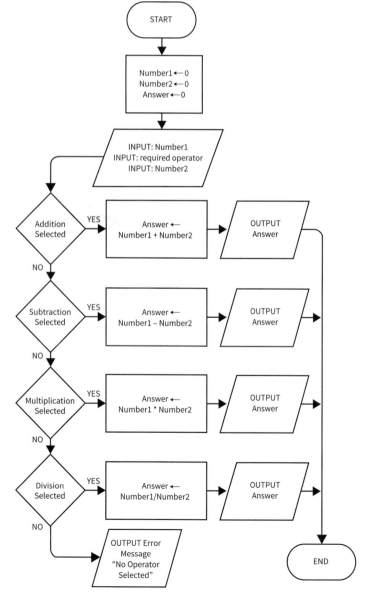

Figure 4.07   Flowchart for Calculator algorithm

```
DECIMAL: Number1 ← 0, Number2 ← 0
STRING: Operator ← ""

INPUT Number1
INPUT Operator
INPUT Number2

CASE Operator
CASE "Add"
        OUTPUT Number1 + Number2
CASE "Subtract"
        OUTPUT Number1 – Number2
CASE "Multiply"
        OUTPUT Number1 * Number2
CASE "Divide"
        OUTPUT Number1 / Number2
OTHERWISE
        OUPUT "Incorrect Operator"
END CASE
```

(a)

```
DECIMAL: Number1 ← 0, Number2 ← 0
STRING: Operator ← ""

INPUT Number1
INPUT Operator
INPUT Number2

IF Operator = "Add" THEN
    OUTPUT Number1 + Number2
ELSE
    IF Operator = "Subtract" THEN
        OUTPUT Number1 – Number2
    ELSE
        IF Operator = "Multiply" THEN
            OUTPUT Number1 * Number2
        ELSE
            IF Operator = "Divide" THEN
                OUTPUT Number1 / Number2
            ELSE
                OUPUT "Incorrect Operator"
            END IF
        END IF
    END IF
END IF
```

(b)

Figure 4.08 Pseudocode for CASE and Nested IF approach to Calculator algorithm

The simplicity of the CASE option (Figure 4.08(a)) is clear to see.

The following code would implement an appropriate Console Application for this task:

```
Module Module1
    Sub Main()
        'Declare local variables
        'Note that Operatorr is misspelt as Operator is a keyword
        'and cannot be used as an identifier
        Dim Number1 As Integer = 0
        Dim Number2 As Integer = 0
        Dim Operatorr As String = ""

        Console.WriteLine("Enter First Number")
        Number1 = Console.ReadLine

        Console.WriteLine("INPUT one of the following options")
        Console.WriteLine("Add")
        Console.WriteLine("Subtract")
        Console.WriteLine("Multiply")
        Console.WriteLine("Divide")
        Operatorr = Console.ReadLine

        Console.WriteLine("Enter Second Number")
        Number2 = Console.ReadLine

        Select Case Operatorr
            Case Is = "Add"
                Console.WriteLine(Number1 + Number2)
            Case Is = "Subtract"
                Console.WriteLine(Number1 – Number2)
            Case Is = "Multiply"
                Console.WriteLine(Number1 * Number2)
```

```
            Case Is = "Divide"
                Console.WriteLine(Number1 / Number2)
            Case Else
                Console.WriteLine("Incorrect Input")
        End Select
        Console.ReadKey()
    End Sub
End Module
```

Although this approach requires the user to input the name of the operator, alternative approaches would work equally efficiently. For example the user could be required to input 1 for Add, 2 for Subtract etc. The CASE statement would then use an Integer variable.

If coded for a Windows Forms Application the user could be offered a GUI to input data. Instead of typing in the required operation name the user could select from a choice of buttons. The design for the interface will need to contain the input and output textboxes, the four operation buttons and an 'equals' button (see Figure 4.09).

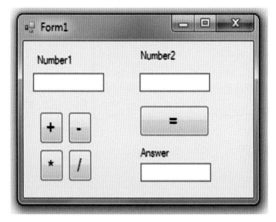

Figure 4.09 Windows Forms calculator interface

Remember to give the design elements appropriate names. You can alter the properties of the buttons to improve the appearance of the interface. This example has used larger text for the operator buttons.

For this system to work the program will need to perform different actions depending on which button is pressed. The buttons will need to change the value of an appropriate variable to indicate the user's choice, while the 'equals' button will perform the mathematical calculation.

The appropriate code will need to be included in the relevant button click event.

```
Public Class Form1

    'Declare and initialise all the required variables
    Dim Operation As Integer = 0
    Dim Num1 As Decimal = 0
    Dim Num2 As Decimal = 0

    Private Sub BTNAdd_Click(sender As Object, e As EventArgs) Handles BTNAdd.Click
        'Sets the variable to 1
        Operation = 1
    End Sub

    Private Sub BTNSubtract_Click(sender As Object, e As EventArgs) Handles BTNSubtract.Click
        'Sets the variable to 2
        Operation = 2
    End Sub
```

```
    Private Sub BTNMultiply_Click(sender As Object, e As EventArgs) Handles BTNMultiply.Click
        'Sets the variable to 3
        Operation = 3
    End Sub

    Private Sub BTNDivide_Click(sender As Object, e As EventArgs) Handles BTNDivide.Click
        'Sets the variable to 4
        Operation = 4
    End Sub

    Private Sub BTNEquals_Click(sender As Object, e As EventArgs) Handles BTNEquals.Click
        'Obtains the values from the input textboxes and stores in the variables
        Num1 = TBNum1.Text
        Num2 = TBNum2.Text

        'A series of IF statements to perform operation depending on variable value
        If Operation = 1 Then
            TBAnswer.Text = Num1 + Num2
        Else

            If Operation = 2 Then
                TBAnswer.Text = Num1 - Num2
            Else

                If Operation = 3 Then
                    TBAnswer.Text = Num1 * Num2
                Else

                    If Operation = 3 Then
                        TBAnswer.Text = Num1 / Num2
                    Else
                        MsgBox("Select Operation")
                    End If
                End If
            End If
        End If

        'Sets variable values to 0 and clears the input textboxes ready for the
        'next calculation. Program would run without this step but it is good practice
        Num1 = 0
        Num2 = 0
        TBNum1.Text = ""
        TBNum2.Text = ""
    End Sub
End Class
```

The code for the calculator's Windows Forms Application makes use of nested IF statements, although CASE statements could also have been used.

4.10 ELSE IF Statements

In Visual Basic, and some other languages, it is possible to write the equivalent of a series of nested IF statements by making use of an ELSE IF statement. It is executed in a similar way but is easier to read:

```
If Operation = 1 Then
    TBAnswer.Text = Num1 + Num2
ElseIf Operation = 2 Then
    TBAnswer.Text = Num1 - Num2
ElseIf Operation = 3 Then
    TBAnswer.Text = Num1 * Num2
ElseIf Operation = 3 Then
    TBAnswer.Text = Num1 / Num2
Else
    MsgBox("Select Operation")
End If
```

The statement is read sequentially, each condition being checked in turn until a condition is found to be true. The code attached to that condition will be run and then the IF statement will be exited.

TIP

It is possible to code a given scenario by making use of any of the selection methods. When deciding on the best method consider the advantages:

- CASE..OF..OTHERWISE..END CASE offers easy to read selection where multiple paths are determined by a single variable or input. Only one path is followed.
- IF..THEN..ELSE..END IF offers a simple solution where only two paths exist. It can have complex criteria consisting of several variables or inputs.
- IF..THEN..ELSE IF..ELSE..END IF allows multiple paths to be considered. It can have complex criteria consisting of several variables or inputs.
- Nested IF allows multiple paths to be considered. Subsequent decisions can be made depending on earlier decisions. It can have complex criteria consisting of several variables or inputs.

All of the options offer a default path for when the data does not meet any of the possible criteria.

Examination Grading System

This program is required to take the input values of the number of marks the students achieved and the total number of marks available in the examination. It will output the grade obtained based on the grade boundaries in Table 4.04.

Figure 4.10 shows the flowchart design of the intended algorithm. Figure 4.11 shows the pseudocode for a nested IF design (Figure 4.11(a)) and a CASE design (Figure 4.11(b)).

Table 4.04

Grade awarded	Condition
A	Student achieves 80% or more of the marks
B	Student achieves 70% or more of the marks
C	Student achieves 60% or more of the marks
U	Student achieves less than 60% of the marks

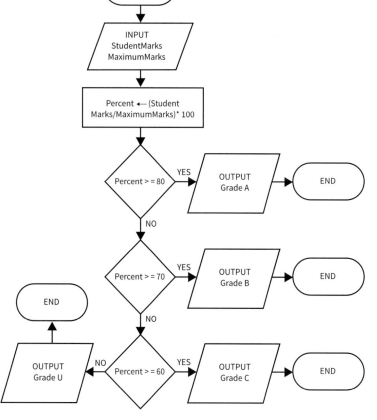

Figure 4.10 Flowchart for Examination Grading System algorithm

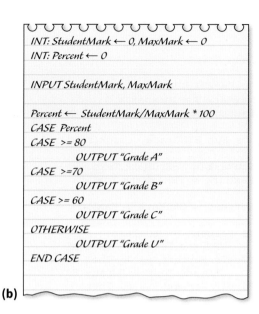

(a)

(b)

Figure 4.11   Pseudocode for Nested IF and CASE approach to Examination Grading algorithm

Figure 4.12 shows a Visual Basic implementation of a Console Application for each of the pseudocode designs. It is crucial that the selection process is completed in the correct order to avoid unexpected results.

Had the algorithm in Figure 4.12(a) been written with the first IF condition set to detect the C grade (at 60%) it would only ever return C or U grades. Any value below 60% would match the Else condition for Grade U while any other value would meet the condition of >= 60 which would then output 'Grade C' and exit the statement.

```
Module Module1
    Sub Main()

        Dim StuMark As Integer = 0
        Dim MaxMark As Integer = 0
        Dim Percent As Integer = 0

        Console.WriteLine("Input STUDENT Mark")
        StuMark = Console.ReadLine
        Console.WriteLine("Input MAX Mark")
        MaxMark = Console.ReadLine

        Percent = StuMark / MaxMark * 100

        If Percent >= 80 Then
            Console.WriteLine("Grade A")
        Else
            If Percent >= 70 Then
                Console.WriteLine("Grade B")
            Else
                If Percent >= 60 Then
                    Console.WriteLine("Grade C")
                Else
                    Console.WriteLine("Grade U")
                End If
            End If
        End If
        Console.ReadKey()
    End Sub
End Module
```

(a)

```
Module Module1
    Sub Main()
        'Declaration of variables
        'NOTE - although Percent is possible to be
        'calculated as a decimal. It has been declared
        'as an Integer to round the calculated value
        'to a whole number
        Dim StuMark As Integer = 0
        Dim MaxMark As Integer = 0
        Dim Percent As Integer = 0

        Console.WriteLine("Input STUDENT Mark")
        StuMark = Console.ReadLine
        Console.WriteLine("Input MAX Mark")
        MaxMark = Console.ReadLine

        Percent = StuMark / MaxMark * 100

        Select Case Percent
            Case Is >= 80
                Console.WriteLine("Grade A")
            Case Is >= 70
                Console.WriteLine("Grade B")
            Case Is >= 60
                Console.WriteLine("Grade C")
            Case Else
                Console.WriteLine("Grade U")
        End Select
        Console.ReadKey()
    End Sub
End Module
```

(b)

Figure 4.12   Visual Basic approach to Examination Grading algorithm

Figure 4.13 shows a Windows Forms Application coded using this IF..ELSE IF statement:

```
Public Class Form1

    Dim StuMark As Integer = 0
    Dim MaxMark As Integer = 0
    Dim Percent As Decimal = 0

    Private Sub BTNGrade_Click(sender As Object, e As EventArgs) Handles BTNGrade.Click

        StuMark = TBStuMark.Text
        MaxMark = TBMaxMark.Text

        Percent = StuMark / MaxMark * 100

        If Percent >= 80 Then
            TBGrade.Text = "Grade A"
        ElseIf Percent >= 70 Then
            TBGrade.Text = "Grade B"
        ElseIf Percent >= 60 Then
            TBGrade.Text = "Grade C"
        Else
            TBGrade.Text = "Grade U"
        End If

    End Sub

End Class
```

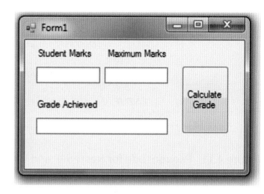

Figure 4.13 Windows Forms interface for Examination Grading algorithm

Parcel Delivery System

A system is required to calculate the delivery cost of parcels. All parcels have a fixed charge for delivery if the parcel is below 5 kg in weight. For local deliveries this charge is $20; for international deliveries the charge raises to $40.

The maximum weight limit for international deliveries is 5 kg, however for local deliveries extra weight is permitted and charged at $1 for every 1 kg above that limit.

1 Draw a flowchart and create a pseudocode algorithm that will identify if the parcel is local or international and then apply the appropriate weight formula to calculate the correct cost.

2 Test that your algorithm works by programming and running the coding in Visual Basic.

CO$_2$ Calculator

A student has been asked to create a simple CO$_2$ calculator. The system is intended to show the difference in emissions between petrol and diesel cars. The intended inputs are the type of fuel the car uses and whether the capacity of the engine is greater than 2 litres. The user will also input the distance travelled in the car in kilometres. The emission values in tonnes of CO$_2$ per 1000 kilometres are shown in Table 4.05.

Table 4.05

Fuel Type	Engine size 2 litres or less	Engine size greater than 2 litres
Petrol	0.208 tonnes CO$_2$/1000 km	0.296 tonnes CO$_2$/1000 km
Diesel	0.176 tonnes CO$_2$/1000 km	0.236 tonnes CO$_2$/1000 km

1 Draw a flowchart and create a pseudocode algorithm that will output the tonnes of CO$_2$ for the distance and type of vehicle input.

2 Test that your algorithms work by programming and running the code in Visual Basic.

Calculator

This task can only be implemented as a Windows Forms Application.

The calculator you have made requires you to input two numbers into two different input textboxes. Most calculators only have one display box for both the input and output. They follow this process:

1 Input first number in display box.
2 Select operator which clears the display box and stores first number.
3 Input second number in display box.
4 Select 'equals' which performs the intended operation and displays result.
5 Select 'clear' which clears stored values and clears the display.

Produce a flowchart and pseudocode to create a program for a calculator that has only one textbox and performs the process described above.

4.10 Connecting Logical Operators

Often a single logical operator is not sufficient to define the required criteria. For example a fire alarm system may be required to activate if it detects either the presence of smoke or a high temperature. The logical operator in this case requires two criteria, either of which being true would cause activation of the alarm.

Visual Basic, in common with many other languages, uses the logical connectors shown in Table 4.06.

Table 4.06

Operator	Description	Example
AND	**All** connected operators must be True for the condition to be met.	IF StudentUser = True **AND** IDNumber > 600 The condition will only be True where the user is a student with an ID number higher than 600. Any other type of user with an ID number > 600 will not meet the criteria because it will fail the StudentUser = True element of the condition.
OR	**Only one** of the connected operators needs to be True for the condition to be met.	IF SmokeDetected = True **OR** Temperature > 70 °C The condition will be True if either smoke is detected or the temperature is above 70 °C. It will also be True if both elements are met.
NOT	Used where it is easier to define the logical criteria in a negative way. Can also be written as <>	IF **NOT** Input_Number = 6 IF Input_Number <> 6 The condition will be True for any number input with the exception of the number 6.

Using AND to Provide Range Criteria

In the following code, the condition is met if the input number is greater than 10 but less than 15.

```
If Num > 10 And Num < 15 Then
     'code to execute
End If
```

Beware of getting the wrong operator. Using OR in the statement would evaluate to true for any number.

Using the AND Operator to Replace a Nested IF Statement

A nested IF statement is often used to check two conditions.

```
If StudentUser = True Then
        If IDNumber > 600 Then
            'Code to execute
        End If
End If
```

If the conditions are simple, the nested IF statement can be replaced by AND. The following code represents the same conditions:

```
If StudentUser = True And IDNumber > 600 Then
        'Code to execute
End If
```

Using Logical Connectors

It is possible to use logical connectors to simplify the complex NESTED IF statement used to code the Parcel Delivery System task. Figure 4.14 shows the simplified flowchart and pseudocode and then there is the Visual Basic implementation.

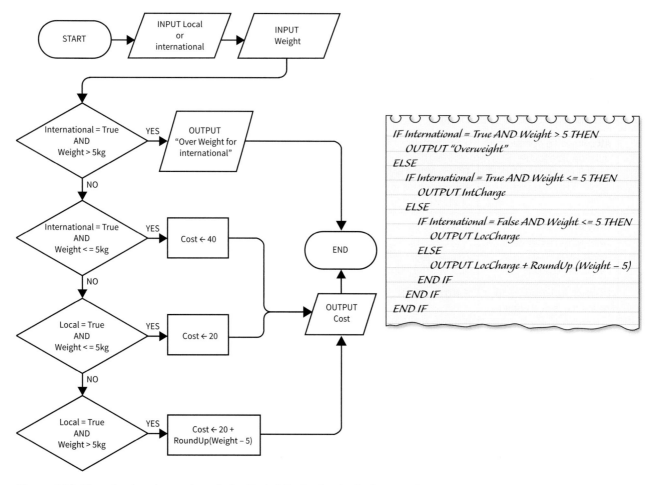

Figure 4.14 Flowchart and pseudocode for Postal Cost using logical connectors

```
Dim International As Integer = 0
Dim Weight As Decimal = 0
Declaring the fixed charges as constants as values will not change
Const IntCharge As Integer = 40
Const LocCharge As Integer = 20

Console.WriteLine("Select Local or International")
Console.WriteLine("1 = Local")
Console.WriteLine("2 = International")
International = Console.ReadLine

Console.WriteLine("Insert Weight")
Weight = Console.ReadLine

If International = 2 And Weight > 5 Then
   Console.WriteLine("Over Weight")
Else
   If International = 2 And Weight <= 5 Then
      Console.WriteLine(IntCharge)
   Else
      If International = 1 And Weight <= 5 Then
         Console.WriteLine(LocCharge)
      Else
         Console.WriteLine(LocCharge + Math.Ceiling(Weight - 5))
      End If
   End If
End If
```

Notice the use of an integer variable 'International' to record the user's selection. It is not uncommon to use an integer variable in this way.

The section of code below shows how the nested IF could have been written as an ELSE IF statement.

```
If International = 2 And Weight > 5 Then
    Console.WriteLine("Over Weight")
ElseIf International = 2 And Weight <= 5 Then
    Console.WriteLine(IntCharge)
ElseIf International <> 2 And Weight <= 5 Then
    Console.WriteLine(LocCharge)
Else
    Console.WriteLine(LocCharge + Math.Ceiling(Weight - 5))
End If
```

Notice that all the IF statements contain two conditions connected with the AND operator.

EXTENSION TASK

CO_2 Calculator

Rewrite the CO_2 emissions program to use connected criteria rather than nested IF statements.

The original calculator program is capable of performing only one arithmetic calculation at a time. Many calculators allow the user to enter a sequence of numbers and operators, displaying the cumulative result of the arithmetic process as the sequence is entered. An example of this process is given in Table 4.07 on page 50.

Table 4.07

User input	Display	Process
43	43	
+	43	• Stores first number input • Records the addition operator selected
11	11	
*	54	• Completes the addition of the stored number with new number (43 + 11) and outputs result (54) • Records that multiplication is the latest operator selected • Stores 54 as the cumulative result
2	2	
–	108	• Completes the multiplication of the cumulative value by the new number input (54 * 2) and outputs the result which is 108 • Records that subtraction is the latest operator selected • Stores 108 as the cumulative result
100	100	
/	8	• Completes the subtraction of the new number from the cumulative value (108 – 100) and outputs the result which is 8 • Records that division is the latest operator selected • Stores 8 as the cumulative result
2	2	
=	4	• Completes the division of the cumulative value by the new number input (8 / 2) and outputs the result which is 4 • Records end of sequence by setting all operator indicators to False • Sets cumulative result and any interim stored numbers to 0

EXTENSION TASK

Calculator

Produce a flowchart and pseudocode for a calculator that is capable of allowing a sequence of numbers and operators to be input. When the first operator is selected it will store the initial value. As subsequent operators are pressed they will complete the previous operation, storing and displaying the cumulative value. The equals button will end the sequence, display the final cumulative value and reset any variables to allow a new sequence to be input.

Test that your algorithms work by programming and running the calculator in Visual Basic.

Summary

- Selection provides methods that programmers can use to allow the algorithm to follow different paths through the code depending on the data being used at the time.
- The flowchart symbol for selection is a decision diamond ◇. The selection criteria are included in the symbol. The exit paths should be indicated as YES and NO or TRUE and FALSE.
- Multiple decisions are shown as a series of connected decisions.
- Logical operators are used to provide a range of comparative options.
- IF statements provide the ability to use complex criteria based on multiple variables or user inputs.
- Nested IF statements provide the ability for additional conditions to be checked once a path has been determined by earlier conditions.
- CASE statements provide a simple method of providing multiple paths based on a single variable or user input.
- The ELSE statement (used with IF) and the OTHERWISE statement (used with Case) provide a default path should none of the conditions be met.

Chapter 5:
Iteration

Learning objectives

By the end of this chapter you will understand:

- the need for iteration
- how to design and represent iteration using flowcharts and pseudocode
- how to write code that will repeat instructions a predetermined number of times
- how to write code that will repeat instructions based on user input
- how to use counters with repeated code
- the advantages and disadvantages of FOR, WHILE and REPEAT UNTIL loops.

5.01 Need for Iteration

Many processes and algorithms will complete repetitive operations on changing data. For example a system that is required to check that a series of 100 numbers are all above a certain value, would be required to check each value against the same condition. It would be impractical to reproduce that code 100 times; a better alternative would be to rerun the same checking algorithm 100 times with the input value changing each time the code is repeated. Another algorithm may be required to evaluate each character in a string; a loop could be used to re-run the evaluation code for each character in the string.

5.02 Types of Iteration

Three basic forms of iteration (see Table 5.01) exist in the majority of programing languages. They are known as 'loops', because they cause the program to repeatedly 'loop through' the same lines of code.

Table 5.01

Loop type	Description	When it should be used
FOR loop	Repeats a section of code a predetermined number of times	The number of iterations is known or can be calculated. The programmer can set the code to loop the correct number of times.
WHILE loop	Repeats a section of code while the control condition is true	The number of iterations is not known and it may be possible that the code will never be required to run. The condition is checked before the code is executed. If the condition is false the code in the loop will not be executed.
REPEAT UNTIL loop	Repeats a section of code until the control condition is true	The number of iterations is not known but the code in the loop must be run at least once. The condition is checked after the code has been executed, so the code will run at least once.

Often it is possible to use any of the three types when producing an algorithm; however each type offers the programmer certain advantages. Selecting the most appropriate type of loop can help to make your code more efficient.

5.03 FOR Loops

A **FOR loop** can only be used where the number of iterations is known at the time of programming. Often this will be in a situation when the number of iterations is 'hard coded' but it is also possible to make use of variables when identifying the number of iterations.

SYLLABUS CHECK

Pseudocode: understand and use pseudocode, using FOR..TO..NEXT loop structures.

These are also known as 'count-controlled' loops because the number of iterations is controlled by a loop counter. It is traditional to use a variable named i (an abbreviation for the word 'index') as the control variable.

When writing a FOR loop in Visual Basic you need to follow this format:

```
For i = 1 To 10
    'Code to execute
Next
```

Each individual element of the loop performs an important role in achieving the iteration as shown in Table 5.02.

Table 5.02

Element	Description
`For`	The start of the loop
`i = 1 To 10`	`i` is a counter variable that records the number of iterations that have been run. This is usually incremented by 1 every iteration. In Visual Basic there is no requirement to declare the counter variable separately – it is automatically declared as part of the FOR loop. The value of the counter variable can be used within the loop to perform incremental calculations.
`Next`	The end of the iteration section
	The value of the counter variable is incremented and the flow of the program goes back to the `For`. The loop will evaluate if the counter value is within the condition (10 in this example). If the counter has exceeded the end value, the loop will direct the flow of the program to the line of code following `Next`; if not it will rerun the loop.

Any code that is placed within the FOR loop will be repeated on each iteration. The repeated code can itself include complex processes such as selection or additional loops.

KEY TERM

FOR loop: A type of iteration that will repeat a section of code a known number of times.

TIP

As the conditions are checked at `For`, `Next` will always pass execution of the loop back to `For` to check the conditions. It is a common misconception that once the maximum number of iterations has been reached `Next` will exit the loop. This is not true. Consider a situation where a FOR loop is written to execute 10 times. Although the loop counter may have reached 10 `Next` will still increment to counter to 11 before passing execution to `For`. The value of the loop counter will be outside the criteria and `For` will then exit the loop.

A system is required to output the multiples of a given number up to a maximum of 10 multiples. For example the multiples of 6 are 6, 12, 18, 24, 30, 36, 42, 48, 54 and 60. Figure 5.01 shows the flowchart and pseudocode for the design of the algorithm. Although the counter is automatically declared in Visual Basic this is not the case with all languages so it is normal to include the declaration in the design.

SYLLABUS CHECK

Pseudocode: understand and use pseudocode for counting (e.g. Count ← Count + 1).

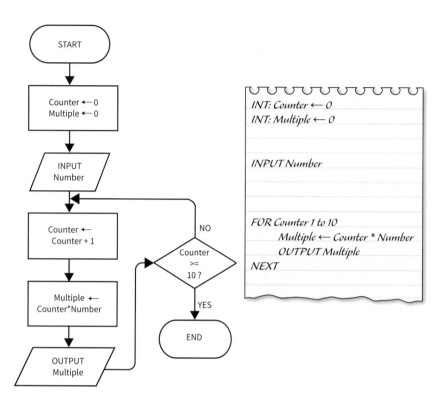

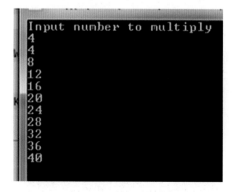

Figure 5.01 Flowchart and pseudocode for outputting multiples

The code for the Console Application in Figure 5.02 could be similar to the following:

```
Module Module1
    Sub Main()
        Dim Multiply As Integer

        Console.WriteLine("Input number to multiply")
        Multiply = Console.ReadLine

        For i = 1 To 10
            Console.WriteLine(Multiply * i)
        Next

        Console.ReadKey()
    End Sub
End Module
```

Figure 5.02 Output of multiples in Console window

The Windows Forms Application in Figure 5.03 makes use of a listbox which will hold multiple string entries as a list of items.

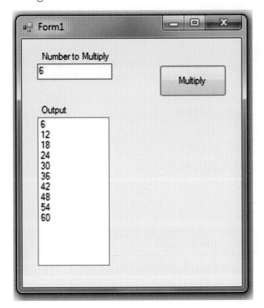

Figure 5.03 Windows Forms application of multiplier

Items are added to the listbox by using the code:

```
ListBoxName.Items.Add(item to add)
```

The item to add can be a textual value enclosed by inverted commas, for example "textual value". Alternatively the name of a variable can be provided in which case the value in the variable is used. The code to achieve Figure 5.03 would be:

```
Public Class Form1
      'Declare and initialise the variable to hold the input number
      Dim Multiply As Integer

      Private Sub BTNMultiply _ Click(sender As Object, e As EventArgs) Handles BTNMultiply.Click
            'Obtain the input value from the textbox and place in the variable
            Multiply = TBInput.Text

            'Start the FOR loop to iterate 10 times
            For i = 1 To 10
                  'Add the calculated multiplication to the list box
                  ListBoxOutput.Items.Add(Multiply * i)
            Next
      End Sub
End Class
```

TASK

FOR Loop

1 Extend the multiply system to include two inputs. The first input is the number to multiply, the second is the number of multiples required.

2 Produce a system that accepts two numbers A and B and outputs A^B. For example if $A = 3$ and $B = 4$, the output will be 81 ($A^4 = A \times A \times A \times A$).

5.04 Using Loops with Advanced Arithmetic Operators

In Chapter 3 we learnt about the use of basic arithmetic operators such as add and divide. Visual Basic offers more advanced arithmetic operators.

A particular example of this is the way in which we divide numbers. It would be normal to expect the result of a division to be an exact value such as 91/24 = 3.792. But if you are dealing with data that can only be represented as integers then a different approach might be needed.

If you had to organise transport for a group of 91 people using buses that can hold a maximum of 24 people you are more likely to want to express 91/24 in the format '3 remainder 19'. This format would allow you to identify that you would need four buses and still have seats available for another five people. The arithmetic terms for these items are 'quotient' and 'modulus' (see Table 5.03) and they prove useful when producing certain mathematical algorithms.

Table 5.03

Operator	Description	Visual Basic code
Quotient	A division operation which outputs the integer part of the result. This is also known as integer division.	Use the backslash symbol (the opposite from the normal divide symbol): 91 \ 24 = 3
Modulus	A division operation which outputs the remainder part of the result. The amount by which one number will not exactly divide into another.	Use the command word 'Mod' 91 Mod 24 = 19

A prime number can only be divided equally by 1 or itself. If a number can divide equally into another number the modulus of that operation will be zero, therefore a prime number can also be defined as a number that when divided by all the positive integers between 1 and itself, will not result in a modulus of zero. We will use this rule to produce an algorithm capable of determining if a number is a prime. Figure 5.04 shows the flowchart and pseudocode for a solution.

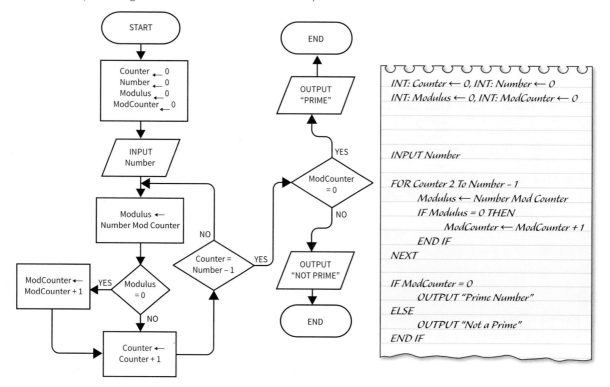

Figure 5.04 Flowchart and pseudocode for the Prime algorithm

NOTE: In both designs the iteration counter starts from 2 and ends at Number – 1 to avoid the use of 1 and the number input in the loop. These would obviously result in a modulus of zero.

TASK

Discussion Question

Is limiting the iterations to Number – 1 the most efficient range limiter? What might be a better option?

The following is the code for a Console Application implementation:

```
Module Module1
    Sub Main()
        'Declare and initialise varaibles
        Dim NumberIn As Integer = 0
        Dim Modulus As Integer = 0
        Dim ModCount As Integer = 0

        Console.WriteLine("Input Number to Test")
        NumberIn = Console.ReadLine

        'Start the loop from 2 to avoid using 1 in the
        'iteration. Range of loop is Number - 1 to avoid
        'using the input number in the iteration
        For i = 2 To NumberIn - 1
            'Modulus for each positive number calculated
            Modulus = NumberIn Mod i
            'IF statement will increment ModCount if the
            'modulus is zero
            If Modulus = 0 Then
                ModCount = ModCount + 1
            End If
        'Next increments the counter and directs execution to FOR
        Next

        'Once FOR loop is complete ModCount is used to
        'identify if input number was prime
        If ModCount = 0 Then
            Console.WriteLine("This is a PRIME number")
        Else
            Console.WriteLine("This is NOT a PRIME number")
        End If
        Console.ReadKey()
    End Sub
End Module
```

For a Windows Forms Application the code would be similar but the GUI could be designed as shown in Figure 5.05. A simple interface should be sufficient to indicate if the number input is a prime.

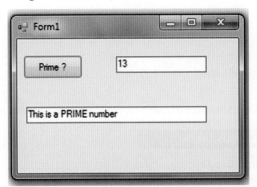

Figure 5.05 Windows Forms applications of primes

57

Change the interface to include a listbox that will output all the positive divisors of the input number in addition to the 'PRIME' or 'NOT PRIME' output. Only show the listbox if the input number is not a prime. You could adapt the following code to achieve this task.

```
Public Class Form1
    Private Sub BTNPrime_Click(sender As Object, e As EventArgs) Handles BTNPrime.Click
            'Declare and initialise the modulus variables
            'Declared locally so reset to zero if user runs code multiple times
        Dim Modulus As Integer = 0
        Dim ModCount As Integer = 0
        Dim NumberIn As Integer = 0

        NumberIn = TBInput.Text

        For i = 2 To NumberIn - 1
            Modulus = NumberIn Mod i
            If Modulus = 0 Then
                ModCount = ModCount + 1
            End If
        Next

        If ModCount = 0 Then
            TBOutput.Text = "This is a PRIME number"
        Else
            TBOutput.Text = "This is a NOT a PRIME number"
        End If
    End Sub
End Class
```

58

5.05 Condition-Controlled Loops

The WHILE..DO..ENDWHILE and REPEAT..UNTIL loop structures are controlled by a specific condition. Iterations are repeated continuously based on certain criteria and allow iteration where the number of repetitions is unknown.

Consider the situation where one random number was constantly subtracted from another until the resultant value was less than zero. It would be impossible to determine the number of iterations required to cause the first number to be less than zero. As a result a FOR loop would not be appropriate; another iterative method would have to be used.

While Loops

Iterations continue while the loop conditions remain true irrespective of the number of iterations this may generate. It is usual for the code within the loop to impact on the conditional values of the loop in such a way that the criteria will eventually become false and the loop will cease.

Because the conditions are tested at the start it is possible that the loop will never run, if the conditions are false at the outset. It is also possible to inadvertently code an infinite loop where the conditions remain true for ever.

When writing a **WHILE loop** in Visual Basic you use the following format:

```
Do While counter > 0

    'code to be iterated'
    counter = counter - 1
Loop
```

SYLLABUS CHECK

Pseudocode: understand and use pseudocode, using WHILE..DO..ENDWHILE loop structures.

Each individual element of the loop performs an important role in achieving the iteration as shown in Table 5.04.

Table 5.04

Element	Description
`Do While`	The start of the loop
`counter > 0`	The condition that controls the loop. Each time the iteration is run the condition is evaluated and if it remains True the iteration will run. Once the condition is False execution of the code is directed to the line following `Loop`. In counter controlled WHILE loops it is important that code is included within the loop to increment or decrement the counter. In a FOR loop the NEXT automatically increments the counter. The same facility does not apply to WHILE loops and as a result the programmer must include appropriate code.
`Loop`	The end of the current iteration. Execution of the program returns to `Do While` so the condition can be re-evaluated and further iterations actioned.

TIP

Notice the placement of `Do`. In pseudocode it is placed after the condition: WHILE 'condition' DO. Visual Basic places it at the beginning: `Do While` 'condition'.

KEY TERM

WHILE loop: A type of iteration that will repeat a sequence of code while a set of criteria continue to be met. If the criteria are not met at the outset the loop will not run and the code within it will not be executed.

The system that was required to output the multiples of a given number up to a maximum of 10 multiples can also be coded making use of a WHILE loop.

Compare the flowchart and pseudocode in Figure 5.06 with the FOR loop example in Figure 5.01.

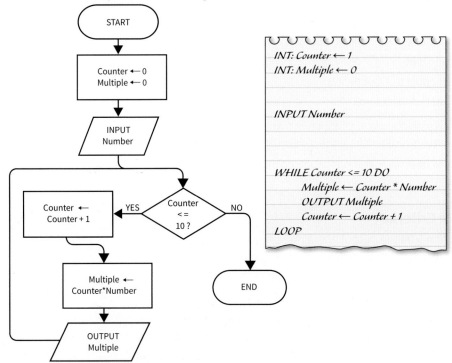

Figure 5.06 Flowchart and pseudocode for a WHILE loop

They follow a largely similar approach but have some significant differences. The logical criteria are reversed in the flowchart.

The format of the WHILE loop has been followed in the pseudocode and the iterated code includes a line which increments the counter.

The following is the code for a Console Application implementation:

```
Module Module1

    Sub Main()
        Dim Multiply As Integer = 0

        'Obtain the input value from the user and place in the variable
        Console.WriteLine("Insert Number")
        Multiply = Console.ReadLine

        'Declare and initialise local variable
        'Initialised to 1 to avoid performing 0 x Input Number
        Dim Counter As Integer = 1

        'Start the while loop - with the condition to loop while counter <= 10
        Do While Counter <= 10
            Console.WriteLine(Multiply * Counter)

            'Increment counter
            'Omit this line and see what happens
            '    it will create an infinite loop because Counter will always be < 10
            Counter = Counter + 1
        Loop
    End Sub
End Module
```

WHILE Loop

TASK

A WHILE loop could be used to calculate the quotient and modulus without using the built-in operators. The WHILE loop would be set to continually subtract number B from number A while number A remains greater than or equal to number B. When this condition is no longer true:

- the number of subtractions is equal to A Quotient B
- the number remaining is equal to A Modulus B.

1 Draw a flowchart and create a pseudocode algorithm that takes as input two numbers and outputs the quotient and modulus resulting from the division of the two numbers.

2 Test that your algorithm works by programming and running the code in Visual Basic.

WHILE Loops with Multiple Criteria

In the prime number task in Section 5.04 the output was a message indicating if the input number was a prime. To achieve this the FOR loop may have iterated many times even though the non-prime nature of the number had already been determined.

For example any even number can be shown not to be prime just by taking the modulus division of 2, making all subsequent iterations unnecessary. A WHILE loop can provide a more efficient solution to the prime number task by looping only while no positive divisor has been tested. The loop can end at the identification of the first positive divisor or when all relevant integer values have been tested.

Problem-solving and design: comment on the effectiveness of a given solution.

To achieve this the WHILE loop will need multiple criteria. In the previous algorithm a count of the number of exact divisors was maintained. In this example a Boolean value is used to indicate that an exact divisor has been identified.

Figure 5.07 shows the flowchart and pseudocode for a solution.

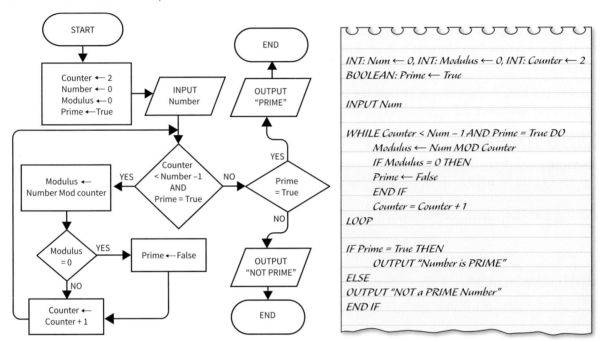

Figure 5.07 Flowchart and pseudocode for WHILE approach

The following is the code for a Console Application implementation:

```
Module Module1
    Sub Main()
        Dim Num As Integer = 0
        Dim Modulus As Integer = 0
        Dim Prime As Boolean = True

        'Obtain and store input from user
        Console.WriteLine("Insert Number to Test")
        Num = Console.ReadLine

        'Declare counter to use with the While loop
        'Initialise to 2 to avoid using 1 as divisor
        Dim Counter As Integer = 2

        'Start the While loop with two conditions
        'The AND connecting operator means BOTH conditions must be True to iterate
        Do While Counter < Num - 1 And Prime = True
            Modulus = Num Mod Counter

            'If statement changes Prime to False if modulus = 0
            'This will cause the loop conditions to be False at next iteration and stop loop
            If Modulus = 0 Then
                Prime = False
            End If
            'Counter incremented to loop through all integer values between 1 and num -1
            Counter = Counter + 1
        Loop
```

```
        'Once loop complete
        'If statement outputs appropriate message based on state of Prime Boolean
        If Prime = True Then
            Console.WriteLine("PRIME number")
        Else
            Console.WriteLine("NOT a PRIME number")
        End If
        Console.ReadKey()
    End Sub
End Module
```

REPEAT..UNTIL Loops

A **REPEAT..UNTIL loop** is very similar to a WHILE loop as iteration will continue based on the loop conditions. It is therefore also able to work in situations where the number of iterations is unknown.

Unlike in a WHILE loop the test is completed at the end of the iteration so the iterated code will always run at least once.

When writing a REPEAT..UNTIL loop in Visual Basic you need to use the following format.

```
Do
        'Code for iteration
        Counter = Counter + 1
Loop Until Counter > 10
```

The individual elements of the code perform an important role in the iteration as shown in Table 5.05.

Table 5.05

Element	Description
Do	The start of the loop.
	At every iteration the execution of the program will be passed to the Do command. Because the loop starts before any conditions are checked the iteration will always run at least once.
Loop Until	The end of the loop.
Counter > 10	The condition for the loop.
	Each time the iteration is run the conditions is evaluated and if it remains False the execution is directed to Do and the iteration will run again. Once the conditions is True the execution of the code is directed to the line following Loop Until.
	It is possible to use the logical operators (AND, OR and NOT) to structure multiple conditions. Counter-based conditions require the counter to incremented by the code contained within the loop.

KEY TERM

REPEAT..UNTIL loop: A type of iteration that will repeat a sequence of code until a certain condition is met.

TIP

Because the check is made at the end of the sequence of code the loop will always run at least once.

The algorithm to calculate if a number is prime can also be coded using a REPEAT..UNTIL loop.

The flowchart and pseudocode for the REPEAT..UNTIL loop are as follows. If you compare these with the WHILE approach in Figure 5.07 your will be able to identify the differences in approach. The decision criteria are checked at different stages during the process, the WHILE at the outset of the loop and the REPEAT..UNTIL at the end. The loop decision for the WHILE is based on the criteria being TRUE and the REPEAT..UNTIL loops if the criteria are FALSE.

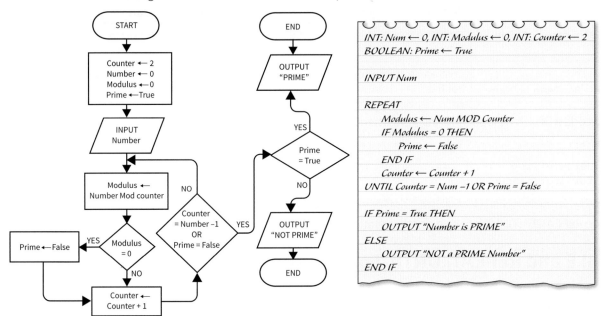

The following is the code for a Console Application implementation:

```
Module Module1
    Sub Main()
        Dim Prime As Boolean = True
        Dim Num As Integer = 0

        Console.WriteLine("Input NUMBER to Test")
        Num = Console.ReadLine

        'Declare counter to use with the UNTIL loop
        'Initialise to 2 to avoid using 1 as divisor
        Dim Counter As Integer = 2

        'Start the Until loop with two conditions that are checked at end
        Do
            'If statement changes Prime to False if modulus = 0
            'This will cause the loop conditions to be False at next check and stop loop
            If Num Mod Counter = 0 Then
                Prime = False
            End If
            'Counter incremented to loop through all integer values between 2 and num - 1
            Counter = Counter + 1
            'Loop Until indicates end of current iteration; conditions are checked
            'The OR connecting operator means EITHER condition could be True to end
            'Both conditions must be False for execution to be passed to the DO
        Loop Until Counter = Num - 1 Or Prime = False

        If Prime = True Then
            Console.WriteLine("PRIME number")
        Else
            Console.WriteLine("NOT a PRIME number")
        End If
        Console.ReadKey()
    End Sub
End Module
```

WHILE and UNTIL Criteria

When considering the criteria for a WHILE or REPEAT..UNTIL loop it is important to remember that the logic for each loop is defined as the opposite of the other. For example if the criteria was based on a Boolean value, the condition would be as shown in Table 5.06.

Table 5.06

Criteria	When Boolean = FALSE	When Boolean = TRUE
`Do While Boolean = False Loop`	Continues to iterate because the Boolean is False.	Ends iteration because the Boolean is not False.
`Do Loop Until Boolean = True`	Continues to iterate because the Boolean is not True.	Ends iteration because the Boolean is True.

It is possible to code a DO UNTIL loop in Visual Basic where the conditions are checked at the outset of the loop:

```
Do Until criteria = True
      'Code for iteration
Loop
```

This is not a true REPEAT..UNTIL loop because of the location of the criteria check.

5.06 WHILE and REPEAT..UNTIL Loops Based on User Input

As both WHILE and REPEAT..UNTIL loops are capable of iterating an unknown number of times, they are able to work in an environment where a user will input a sequence of data items and indicate the end of the sequence by inputting a specific item. Often the data items will be a series of positive numbers and the input that will end the series a negative number.

For example a student is completing an experiment in which they record the height and gender of all the students who they meet in a certain time period. They will indicate the end of the input process by entering a negative value for height. The program will record the average height for each gender and the total number of records entered.

In this scenario the input would be placed within either a WHILE or a REPEAT..UNTIL loop with the loop condition being based on the height input value. The algorithm to maintain the total number of records entered and the height averages would iterate in the loop. The output of the system would most likely be programmed to display only when the loop had ended.

In a Windows Forms Application it is difficult to recreate this type of scenario because the event-driven nature of the language makes the inclusion of input within a loop impossible. However Console mode can be used to show how these types of program can be written and executed.

TIP

When using iteration based on user input it is crucial that the input is included within the loop. A common error is to include a single input outside the loop:

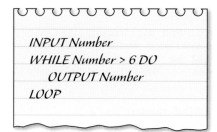

```
INPUT Number
WHILE Number > 6 DO
    OUTPUT Number
LOOP
```

Consider the situation if the user input the number 10. The loop will continually check against the value of 10 and run an infinite number of times. This is known as an infinite loop.

Pseudocode: understand and use pseudocode for totalling (e.g. Sum ← Sum + Number).

A system is required which will allow a user to input a series of positive numbers indicating the end of the sequence by inputting a value of –1. The system will output the sum of the positive numbers input.

The flowchart in Figure 5.08 does not indicate either a WHILE or REPEAT..UNTIL loop – it simply includes the criteria in the loop.

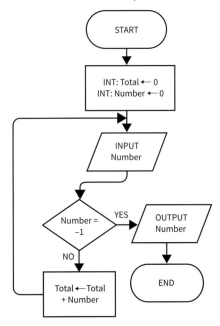

Figure 5.08 Flowchart for input loop

The different approaches can be seen in the pseudocode.

- The WHILE loop (Figure 5.09(a)) requires the first number to be input outside the loop to provide a value to check.

- The REPEAT..UNTIL loop (Figure 5.09(b)) will have included the input of –1 in Total as the conditions are not checked until after the processing in the loop has been completed. Consequently the total has to be recalculated after the loop.

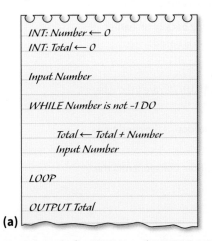

```
INT: Number ← 0
INT: Total ← 0

Input Number

WHILE Number is not -1 DO

    Total ← Total + Number
    Input Number

LOOP

OUTPUT Total
```
(a)

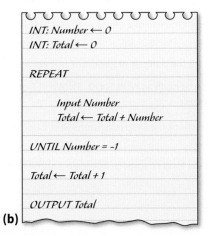

```
INT: Number ← 0
INT: Total ← 0

REPEAT

    Input Number
    Total ← Total + Number

UNTIL Number = -1

Total ← Total + 1

OUTPUT Total
```
(b)

Figure 5.09 Pseudocode for WHILE and REPEAT..UNTIL

Figure 5.10 shows the code for a Console Application implementation using a WHILE loop (Figure 5.10(a)) and a REPEAT..UNTIL loop (Figure 5.10(b)).

```
Module Module1
    'Declare and initialise variables
    Dim Number As Integer = 0
    Dim Total As Integer = 0

    Sub Main()

        'Output to screen input instructions
        Console.WriteLine("Please input a Number")
        Console.WriteLine("Input -1 to End Input Sequence")

        'Obtain first input value
        Number = Console.ReadLine

        'Start loop and check if input is -1
        Do While Number <> -1

            'Increment Total to maintain a sum of numbers input
            Total = Total + Number

            'Output instructions and obtain next input value
            Console.WriteLine("Please input a Number")
            Console.WriteLine("Input -1 to End Input Sequence")
            Number = Console.ReadLine
            'Indicate end of loop and redirects execution to
            'start of the WHILE loop
        Loop

        'Output the value within the variable Total
        Console.WriteLine(Total)
        'Used to hold Total in display until a key pressed
        Console.ReadKey()

    End Sub

End Module
```
(a)

```
Module Module1
    'Declare and initialise variables
    Dim Number As Integer = 0
    Dim Total As Integer = 0

    Sub Main()

        Do
            'Output instructions and obtain input value
            Console.WriteLine("Please input a Number")
            Console.WriteLine("Input -1 to End Input Sequence")
            Number = Console.ReadLine

            'Increment Total to maintain sum of numbers
            Total = Total + Number

            'Indicate end of loop and redirects execution
            'to start of the UNTIL loop
        Loop Until Number = -1

        'Increase Total by 1 as the -1 input was included
        'in Total because the condition is checked
        'after the processing
        Total = Total + 1

        'Output the value within the variable Total
        Console.WriteLine(Total)
        'Used to hold Total in display until a key pressed
        Console.ReadKey()

    End Sub

End Module
```
(b)

Figure 5.10 Visual Basic code for WHILE and REPEAT..UNTIL approach

Summary

- Iteration provides methods that programmers can use to loop through sequences of code multiple times.

- Flowcharts symbolise loops through the use of a decision with a flow line looping back to an earlier element of the diagram. The decision contains the criteria on which the iteration is based.

- A FOR..TO..NEXT loop is used where the number of iterations is known at the outset.

- Condition-controlled loop structures, such as WHILE..DO..ENDWHILE or REPEAT..UNTIL, are used where the number of iterations is unknowns.

- WHILE..DO..ENDWHILE structures check the loop conditions at the outset of the loop. If the conditions are False the loop will never run.

- REPEAT..UNTIL structures check the loop conditions at the end of the first iteration. Consequently the loop will always run at least once.

Chapter 6:
Designing Algorithms

Learning objectives

By the end of this chapter you will understand:

- and be able to apply top-down design
- the format of structure diagrams
- how to combine the constructs of sequence, selection and iteration to design complex systems.

6.01 The Approach

When designing algorithms you will be making use of logical or computational thinking. This requires the ability to analyse a scenario-based task, identify the individual elements of the task and use programming concepts to create an appropriate algorithm. Often more than one approach to a given scenario would produce a working solution which makes this process exciting. Identifying and designing an efficient solution to a problem is at the heart of computational thinking.

> **SYLLABUS CHECK**
>
> **Problem solving and design:** use top-down design and structure diagrams.

6.02 Top-Down Design

Top-down design is an approach to structured programming where the problem is defined in simple steps or tasks. Each of these tasks may be split into a number of smaller subtasks. The process is complete once the problem has been broken down sufficiently to allow it to be understood and programmed. This process is also known as 'step-wise refinement'.

The main advantage of designing in this way is that the final process will be well structured and easier to understand. It can also increase the speed of development as different subtasks can be given to individual members of a programming team. It also helps when debugging or modifying as changes can be made to individual subtasks without necessarily having to change the overall program.

This approach is effective in solving large real-world problems as well as the type of scenario-based questions you may meet during an examination.

6.03 Structure Diagrams

Developed by M. A. Jackson in the 1970s, structure diagrams form part of a method of designing systems known as Jackson Structured Programming (JSP). The method makes use of diagrammatic representations of the programming constructs of sequence, selection and iteration to help design and refine a task into a series of subtasks. The diagrams use the symbols shown in Table 6.01.

Table 6.01

Symbol	Meaning	Description
	Sequence	Each process is represented by a rectangle. The process is identified by the text in the rectangle. The sequence is read left to right. Each subtask is represented by a new layer.
	Selection	Selection is indicated by a circle in the top right of the rectangle. To avoid complex diagrams that become difficult to read it would be normal to have a separate diagram for each of the options.
	Iteration	Iteration is indicated by a star in the top right of the rectangle. Iteration needs an exit condition to avoid becoming an infinite loop.

A school requires a system that will check if students are present in lessons and report to parents any absence. The teacher will record if students are in the lesson and then transfer the record to the school administration team. They will contact parents if students are absent. The process of reporting to parents can be done either by telephone or email.

A good strategy is to consider the situation in terms of the steps of a computer model: Input → Storage → Process → Output.

We could start the design by considering the main elements of the required system:

- The main input will be the record of the students' presence.

- To store this some form of list could be used.

- The process will involve the following sequence of steps:

1 recording the presence of every student who attends the lesson (this will be an iterative process)

2 passing the list to the administration team who will contact parents.

Figure 6.01 shows the initial structure diagram for this system.

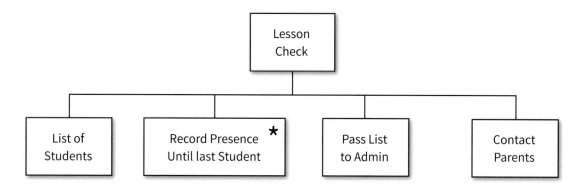

Figure 6.01 Initial structure diagram

The next step is to consider if any of the tasks could be broken down into subtasks. Creating the 'List of Students' is a high-level task that could be broken down into subtasks. Contacting parents can be done by telephone or email and will therefore need subtasks. Figure 6.02 shows the amended structure diagram with these subtasks.

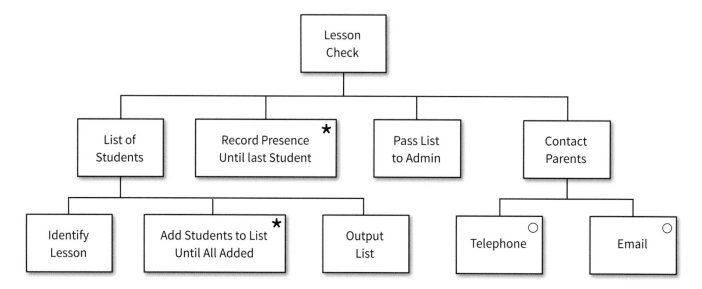

Figure 6.02 Structure diagram showing subtasks

The diagram may not yet be completed. The process 'Identify Lesson' could be broken into subtasks. What inputs would be needed? Where is the data about which students attend the lesson stored? How will the system access those records? This and other tasks would require consideration if this was a real-life scenario.

6.04 Design Steps

As suggested above splitting the overall task into subtasks can be done following the Input → Storage → Process → Output computer model. When designing an algorithm I recommend a slight adaption of that process.

1 Identify the inputs and outputs that are involved in the scenario. At this stage I would consider and make a list of possible variables and data types.

2 For each input identify if the task requires this input to be repeated. This will mean some form of iteration is required. Identify the most appropriate form of iteration.

3 For each output identify the required calculation or recording process required to produce the output value.

   a Does the process involve any decision making? This could mean use of an IF statement.

   b Does the process involve repeated calculation? This could mean some form of iteration.

4 Consider the sequence in which the various subtasks need to be completed:

   • Check that inputs or processes that need to be iterated are within the loop.

   • Check that single inputs and outputs are outside the loop.

   • Check any iteration repeats as expected.

   • Check you have defined and initialised the variables or constants that are to be used.

Considering the inputs and outputs at the start will help you to consider the aim of the system. If you don't consider the required outputs early in the design stage how can you define the process required to produce the outputs?

While I do consider the required variables at the outset of the process I tend to finalise them as a last step to make sure I have not missed any.

TIP

When programming the IDE will alert you to incorrect statements and missing variables. When designing in pseudocode this support is not available. Always check that you have declared and initialised variables correctly and that program statements are complete.

SYLLABUS CHECK

Problem solving and design: produce an algorithm for a given scenario in the form of a flowchart or pseudocode.

Design: Known Quantity of Inputs

A user will input 100 positive numbers into a system. The system will output the highest number and the sum of the numbers input. Design an appropriate algorithm.

Figure 6.03 outlines the computational thinking process for designing the algorithm using the steps described above.

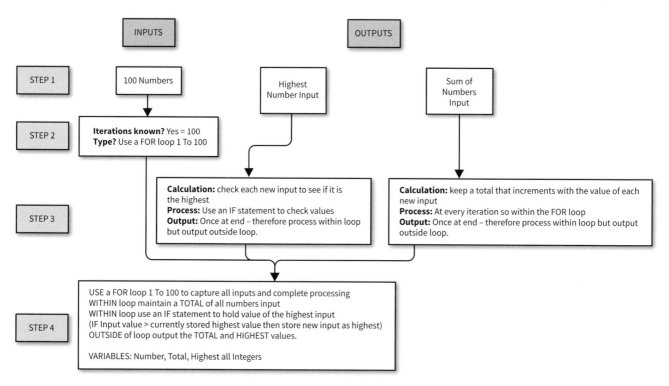

Figure 6.03 The steps in computational thinking

The structure diagram in Figure 6.04 shows the design of the process.

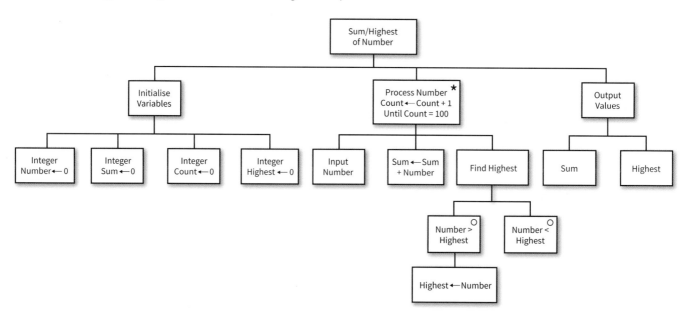

Figure 6.04 Structure diagram

The resultant flowchart and pseudocode are shown in Figure 6.05.

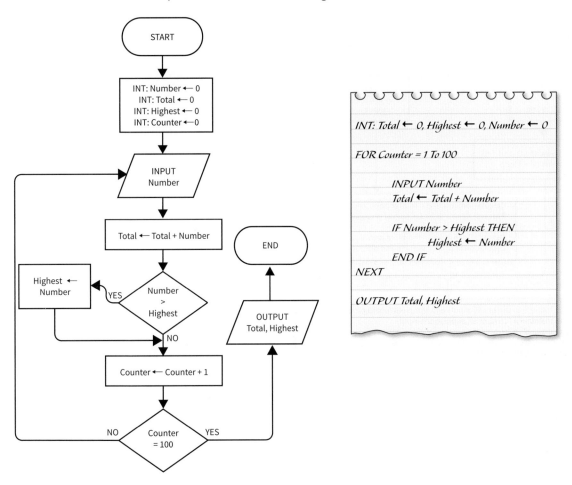

```
INT: Total ← 0, Highest ← 0, Number ← 0

FOR Counter = 1 To 100

        INPUT Number
        Total ← Total + Number

        IF Number > Highest THEN
                Highest ← Number
        END IF
NEXT

OUTPUT Total, Highest
```

Figure 6.05 Flowchart and pseudocode approach

TASK

Discussion Question

This is not the only acceptable solution. Identify other ways this algorithm could have been written.

Design: Unknown Quantity of Inputs

A user is required to input the population of a number of local cities. They will indicate the end of the input sequence by inputting a negative value. The system will output the average population of the cities input.

Figure 6.06 outlines the computational thinking process for designing the algorithm.

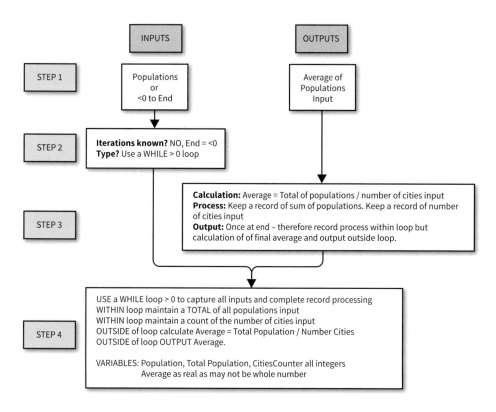

Figure 6.06 Computational thinks steps

The structure diagram in Figure 6.07 shows the design of the process.

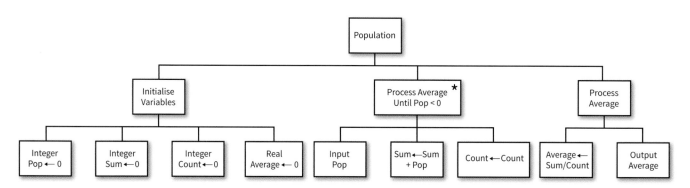

Figure 6.07 Structure diagram

The resultant flowchart and pseudocode are shown in Figure 6.08.

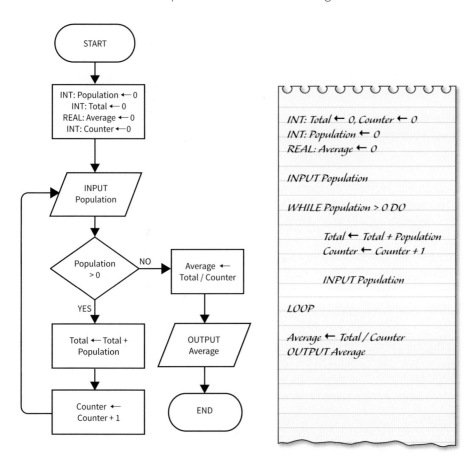

Figure 6.08 Flowchart and pseudocode for Population algorithm

TIP

To check that your solution works as intended it should be tested. See Chapter 9 to discover how this can be achieved.

Design Challenges

The following is a series of examination-style tasks.

For each task, design an appropriate algorithm using a flowchart and pseudocode. Examples of working algorithms are included in Chapter 13 but remember these are not the only possible solutions.

1 A student is completing a mathematical probability study. They are required to throw a standard six-sided dice 100 times. They will input the number shown at each throw into a system. The system will output the number of times the dice shows a six and the average value of all the throws.

2 The student completing the mathematical probability study decides to extend the study to include two standard six-sided dice. The student will throw both dice simultaneously inputting both numbers shown at each throw into a system. The system will record the number of 'doubles' (throws that result in both dice showing the same number). The process will end when 100 doubles have been recorded at which time the system will output the percentage of total throws that resulted in a double.

3 A user inputs into a system a sequence of positive numbers. They indicate the end of the sequence by inputting the value –1. They system will output the highest and lowest numbers input.

4 A user has been asked to investigate the numbers of students that are studying at schools in a geographical region. The user is required to input the name of the school and the number of its students for all 200 schools in the region. The system will output the name of the school with the highest number of students and the name of the school with the lowest number of students.

5 A scientist is using a temperature sensor to record the exothermic reaction caused when he mixes two chemicals. Both chemicals start at the same temperature (which is recorded in the system). Once every minute the sensor sends the temperature of the combined chemicals to the system. The system will continue to record the temperature values as long as the temperature remains above the initial start temperature. The expected output is the length of time in minutes the reaction takes to return to the initial value. It should also show the highest temperature reached and the time, in minutes from the start of the experiment, that this temperature was reached.

Summary

- Systems are made up of subsystems which may in turn be made up of further subsystems.

- Top-down design is a method of simplifying the main system into its subsystems until the system is sufficiently defined to allow it to be understood and programmed.

- Structure diagrams are a diagrammatical method of expressing a system as a series of subsystems.

- When designing solutions for a given problem adopting an Input → Storage → Process → Output approach can help to design an effective solution.

Chapter 7:
Subroutines

Learning objectives

By the end of this chapter you will understand:

- how subroutines are used in programming
- how values are passed to and received from subroutines
- how to design, program and use a function
- how to design, program and use a procedure.

7.01 Subroutines

A subroutine is a sequence of program code that performs a specific task but does not represent the entire system. Subroutines are usually separate modules that you have identified after applying the top-down design technique and producing a structure diagram.

Visual Basic makes extensive use of subroutines and you have already met IDE-generated subroutines.

When using Console mode the system generates a main subroutine which will automatically run when the program is executed. All the code included within the subroutine is executed when the program is run.

```
Sub Main()
    'Code to run
End Sub
```

In many languages the main program is not defined as a separate program.

The Windows Forms mode sets up individual subroutines for each event that is required, for example a button click. The code within the event subroutine will be executed when the event is triggered.

```
Private Sub Button1 _ Click(sender As Object, e As EventArgs) Handles Button1.Click
    'Code to run
End Sub
```

Although they look different these subroutines have a number of common factors:

- They run the code contained within the subroutine when they are activated or called from another routine or the main program.

- They have a beginning indicated by the keyword Sub and an end indicated by the keyword End Sub.

When a subroutine is activated (this is known as 'called'), the calling program or subroutine is halted and control is transferred to the called subroutine. After the subroutine has completed execution control is passed back to the calling program. This modularised approach to programming brings with it advantages over a simple sequenced program.

Consider a Windows Forms program, which maintains its running status while waiting for various subroutines to be called by activation of event triggers. The subroutines execute their code and pass control back to the main program.

This allows the programmer to generate the complete program from a series of individual subroutines. Some code is executed when the form is loaded, other elements when certain buttons are clicked and possibly other elements of code are activated when text is changed in a text box. Image the complexity of the program code if only a single sequence of code was available to the programmer.

SYLLABUS CHECK

Programming concepts: use predefined procedures or functions.

Using Subroutines

Subroutines are clearly a useful tool to the programmer but so far we have only used the subroutines generated by the IDE. It is possible to generate your own subroutines which you can call from the main code. This offers a number of advantages:

- **The subroutine can be called when needed:** A single block of code can be used many times in the entire program, avoiding the need for repeating identical code sequences throughout the overall code. This improves the modularity of the code, makes it easier to understand and helps in the identification of errors.

- **There is only one section of code to debug:** If an error is located in a subroutine only the individual subroutine needs to be debugged. Had the code been repeated through the main program each occurrence would need to be altered.

- **There is only one section of code to update:** Improvements and extensions of the code are available everywhere the subroutine is called.

Types of Subroutine

Two main types of subroutine exist. Both perform tasks that are useful to the user or calling program. Their use can overlap but they do have specific features.

A **procedure** is capable of receiving and returning multiple data values. The data values are passed via parameters which are set up when the procedure is defined. A parameter is information about the data and can be either an actual data item or the identifier of a variable that holds the data item.

The calling program will provide parameter values that will be used by the procedure during its execution. The procedure may use the parameters to complete a task without returning any value to the calling program. Alternatively it may return values resulting from its execution to the calling program. In this situation the calling program will also pass references to the procedure indicating the variable or location to which it should pass the return values.

A **function** is capable of receiving multiple parameters. It will always return a single value. Unlike a procedure, a function always returns a value through its identifier.

The calling program will call a function and pass the required parameters. The function will complete execution and return a single value. This value is handled in the same way that a value from a variable is assigned.

KEY TERM

Procedure: A subroutine that can receive and return multiple parameters. It may or may not return a value. If values are returned they are returned via parameters.

Function: A subroutine that can receive multiple parameters and returns a single value. A function always returns a value through its identifier.

7.02 Programming a Procedure

The syntax for setting up a procedure in Visual Basic is shown in Figure 7.01. A subroutine cannot form part of another routine so the entire code must fall within the class or module but outside any other subroutines. The pseudocode syntax is identical to the programming code.

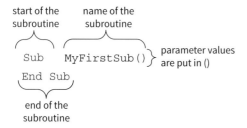

Figure 7.01 Visual Basic syntax for a Procedure

Passing Parameters to a Procedure

The passing of parameters can be very useful. For example, a procedure to check network logon details could take the parameters Username and Password. Having checked the data against the logon database it could return True or False to indicate if details match records, or 'Update Password' if the usage period for a password has expired. The procedure could be called repeatedly and passed different parameters every time a user attempts to log on.

The required parameters are defined within the brackets in the procedure code. Each parameter requires an identifier (name) and it is normal to indicate the data type of the parameter.

Parameters can be passed by value or by reference. If data is passed by value a local copy of the data is held by the procedure and is discarded after the procedure exits. If the data is passed by reference the location in memory, normally a variable identifier, is used by the procedure. Changes to that location are maintained when the procedure exits.

In Visual Basic the required method of passing parameters is indicated by the keywords described in Table 7.01.

Table 7.01

Keyword	Use	Description
ByVal	ByVal Number As Integer	ByVal indicates the parameter is passed by value. Number is the identifier used within the procedure. The procedure will store a local copy of the data passed in Number. The variable Number cannot be accessed outside the procedure.
ByRef	ByRef Output As String	ByRef indicates the parameter is passed by reference. Output is the identifier used within the procedure to hold values; it will update any value in the reference passed from the calling program.

Parameters that are to be returned need to be passed by reference (prefixed by the keyword ByRef in Visual Basic). The order of the parameters is not important but they need to be called in the same order they are defined.

A procedure will be passed an integer value and output the first five multiples of that value. For example, if it is passed 4, it will output the sequence 4, 8, 12, 16 and 20. The pseudocode for the procedure and its calls from the main program are as follows:

```
SUB Multiply(INT: Number)
    FOR i = 1 To 5
        OUTPUT Number * i
    NEXT
END SUB


CALL Multiply(10)
INPUT NumberToMultiply
CALL Multiply(NumberToMultiply)
```

TIP

If the ByVal or ByRef is omitted the default is that the parameter is passed by value. It is possible to omit the ByVal - the procedure Multiply could have been defined as `Sub Multiply(Number As Integer)`. Where a value is to be return the inclusion of the ByRef is vital.

The pseudocode shows two ways of calling the procedure: first it is called with the number 10 as a parameter; more normally, a value contained in a variable or textbox, such as NumberToMultiply, is passed. This gives the ability for the user to change the parameter value.

The Visual Basic code for the procedure is similar to the pseudocode:

```
Module Module1
    Sub Main()
        'Declare and obtain the input number
        Dim NumberToMultiply As Integer
        NumberToMultiply = Console.ReadLine

        'Call the procedure passing the required parameter
        'as the value held within the variable
        'The procedure will run before passing control back
        'to the main subroutine
        Call Multiply(NumberToMultiply)
        Console.ReadKey()
    End Sub

    Sub Multiply(ByVal Number As Integer)
        For i = 1 To 5
            Console.WriteLine(Number * i)
        Next

    End Sub
End Module
```

TASK

Produce Multiples

Create a pseudocode algorithm for an amended version of this procedure that accepts two parameters: one number to use as the multiplier and a second number to indicate the maximum number of multiplications required.

Test that your algorithm works by programming and running the code in Visual Basic.

Returning Parameter Values to the Calling Routine

The procedures used so far have not returned any parameter values to the calling routine. To indicate that a parameter is to be returned it must be prefixed by the keyword `ByRef`. This indicates that the procedure is being given a reference and is expected to alter the value in the variable given as part of the procedure's processing.

A procedure will be passed a value that represents the radius of a circle. It is required to return a value which represents the circumference of the circle defined by the given radius.

The pseudocode solution for both the procedure and the calling routine. Note the use of `ByRef` to indicate a return parameter.

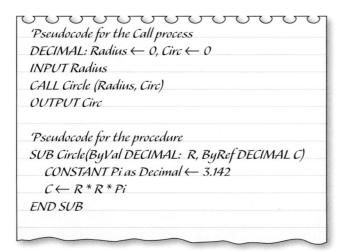

```
'Pseudocode for the Call process
DECIMAL: Radius ← 0, Circ ← 0
INPUT Radius
CALL Circle (Radius, Circ)
OUTPUT Circ


'Pseudocode for the procedure
SUB Circle(ByVal DECIMAL: R, ByRef DECIMAL C)
    CONSTANT Pi as Decimal ← 3.142
    C ← R * R * Pi
END SUB
```

TIP

As this procedure returns one value it could have been programmed as a function.

The Visual Basic code for the procedure is similar to the pseudocode:

```vbnet
Module Module1
    Sub Main()
        Dim Radius, Circ As Decimal

        Console.WriteLine("Insert value of radius")
        Radius = Console.ReadLine
        'Call the procedure providing required parameters
        Call Circle(Radius, Circ)

        Console.WriteLine(Circ)
        Console.ReadKey()

    End Sub

    'Define the procedure
    'Note the use of ByRef to indicate a required return parameter
    'The procedure will:
    '- receive the parameter value R
    '- complete the processing to calculate C
    '- return the value of C by updating the value held in the variable Circ.
    Sub Circle(ByVal R As Decimal, ByRef C As Decimal)
        Const Pi As Decimal = 3.142
        C = R * R * Pi
    End Sub
End Module
```

Circumference and Area

Create a pseudocode algorithm for an amended version of this procedure that returns both the area and the circumference of the circle defined by the radius given.

Test that your algorithm works by programming and running the code in Visual Basic.

7.03 Programming a Function

A function is similar to a procedure but it must return one, and only one, value. It is possible for a procedure to return one parameter so the functionality of these two types of subroutines can overlap.

To show the differing syntax between functions and procedures, we will repeat the example to produce the circumference of a circle given its radius using a function.

Defining a Function

The Visual Basic syntax for defining a function is shown in Figure 7.02:

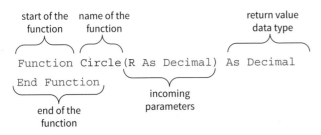

Figure 7.02 Visual Basic syntax for a Function

As a function must return one value there is no need to provide a return reference variable but the return data type is defined. The function identifier behaves like a variable and needs to have a clear reference to the data type it is expected to hold.

A function must also include specific code to return the data. This can be achieved in two ways as shown in Figure 7.03. You can use the keyword `Return` to indicate which value is to be returned (Figure 7.03(a)) or you can use the identifier of the function to hold the return value (Figure 7.03(b)).

```
Function Circle(R As Decimal) As Decimal
    Const Pi As Decimal = 3.142
    Dim C As Decimal
    C = R * R * Pi
    Return C
End Function
```
(a)

```
Function Circle(R As Decimal) As Decimal
    Const Pi As Decimal = 3.142
    Circle = R * R * Pi
End Function
```
(b)

Figure 7.03 Function showing alternative methods of returning values

83

Calling a Function

A function is not activated by use of the keyword `Call`. The name of the function is used as a variable in an assignment statement. Each time the name is used the function is executed and the return value placed in the variable or output indicated.

The following code shows two uses of the Circle function:

```
Sub Main()
        Dim Radius As Decimal = 0
        Dim Circ As Decimal = 0

        Console.WriteLine("Insert value of radius")
        Radius = Console.ReadLine

        Circ = Circle(Radius)
        Console.WriteLine(Circ)

        Console.WriteLine(Circle(Radius))

        Console.ReadKey()
End Sub
```

In the first instance, the value is assigned to a variable called Circ. In the second, the value is passed directly to the Console.WriteLine command.

Summary

- Subroutines provide an independent section of code that be called from another routine while the program is running. In this way subroutines can be used to perform common tasks within a program.

- As an independent section of code, a subroutine is easier to debug, maintain or update than repetitive code within the main program.

- Subroutines are called from another routine. Once they have completed execution they pass control back to the calling routine.

- Subroutines can be passed values known as parameters.

- A procedure is capable of receiving and returning multiple parameters. It may, or may not return a value. If values are returned they are returned via a parameter.

- A function is a type of subroutine which can receive multiple parameters. It always returns a single value through its identifier.

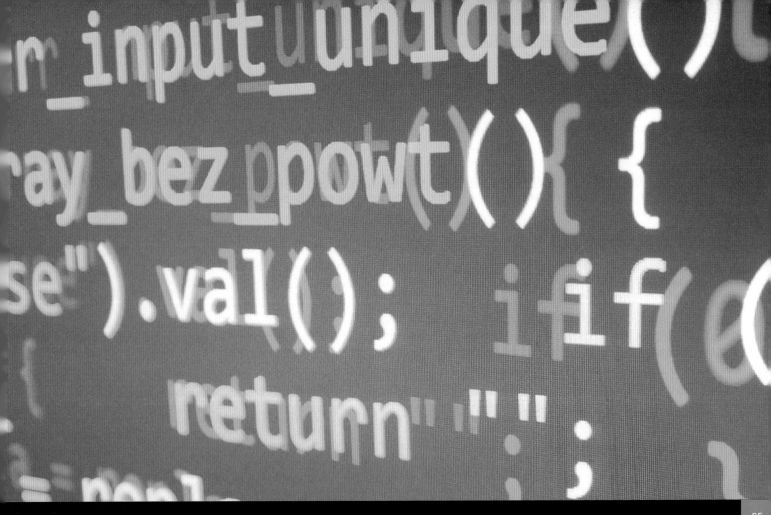

Chapter 8:
Checking Inputs

Learning objectives

By the end of this chapter you will understand:

- the need for accuracy in inputs
- how to design validation routines using flowcharts or pseudocode
- the role and use of a range of validation techniques:
  - presence check
  - range check
  - length check
  - type check
  - format check
  - check digit
- how to program validation techniques into your algorithms.

8.01 The Need for Accuracy

Organisations rely on the accuracy of their data when making decisions. Inaccurate data can compromise the validity of those decisions possibly with devastating results. Consider the situation of doctors receiving inaccurate medical data about patients, or fire fighters being given inaccurate data about wind speed and direction. The largest source of inaccuracies is the data entry process and it is important that systems are designed to help increase the accuracy of data entry.

8.02 Validation

Validation is the process of programming a system to automatically check that data entered meets a set of criteria. Data that falls outside the criteria will be invalid. While validation cannot guarantee that data entered are accurate it does ensure that the data are reasonable and is able to filter out obvious mistakes. For example if a system was recording the height of students it would be reasonable to expect that no student would be more than 3 metres tall. Programming the system to reject data entries above 3 metres would help to remove obvious errors. However if a student's height was measured at 1.4 metres, but inaccurately entered as 1.06, the system would still be accept the value because it meets the validation criteria.

> **SYLLABUS CHECK**
>
> **Problem-solving and design:** understand the need for validation checks to be made on input data.

> **TIP**
> Validation does not make data input accurate – this is a common misconception.

Table 8.01 shows different types of validation checks:

Table 8.01

Validation Type	Description	Example
Presence check	Checks that certain mandatory data has been input. Will reject groups of data where fields have been left blank. Often used with data collection forms.	Online order where 'Email Address' must be provided.
Range check	Checks data falls within a reasonable range. Will reject any data items outside of the expected range. Normally, but not exclusively, used with numeric data. It is possible to have data where the range limit is only applicable to one extreme. For example the volume of a vessel cannot be zero but may not have an upper limit. This is known as a 'limit check'.	Age must be between 0 and 130. Day of the month must be between 1 and 31. Percentage score in an exam must be between 0 and 100.
Length check	Checks that data entered is of a reasonable length. It will reject any data items that have a length outside of the expected values. Normally used with text-based inputs.	Surname must be between 1 and 25 characters long. A password must have more than 6 characters.
Type check (character check)	Checks that a data item is of a particular data type. It will reject any input that is of a different type.	Stock items must be entered as an integer. Age will be numeric (e.g. it will not accept 'over 21').
Format check	Checks that a data item matches a predetermined pattern and that the individual elements of the data item have particular values or data types.	Date of birth will be in the format dd/mm/yyyy. Mobile telephone number will be in the format NNNNN NNNNNN where N is a digit.
Check digit	Checks that a numerical data item has been entered accurately. Extra digit(s) are added to the number based on a calculation that can be repeated, enabling the number to be checked by repeating the calculation and comparing the calculated check digit with the value entered.	A barcode includes a check digit. IBSNs (book numbers) include a check digit.

8.03 Verification

Verification confirms the integrity of data as it is input into the system at the user interface or when it is transferred between different parts of a system. Data integrity is a term that describes the correctness of data during and after processing. Although the format of the data may be changed by processing, if data integrity has been maintained the data will remain a true and accurate representation of the original. Copying data should clearly not change the data values.

Most verification techniques are undertaken by the person inputting the data and involve the checking of the data input into the system against the original. One form of verification that you could program is 'double entry' verification. The data item is entered twice, often by different operators; the system compares the input values and identifies any differences.

8.04 Programming Validation into your Systems

Running code without passing the correct values to the variables will cause a program to crash or provide unexpected results. Run any of your programs without inputting the required numeric values and you will receive the error message shown in Figure 8.01.

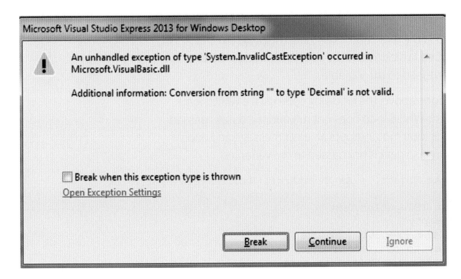

Figure 8.01 Invalid data type error message

As no value was input the system has taken the empty input as an empty string value. It is not possible to convert an empty string to a numeric value causing an unhandled exception error. Should this happen in a published program the system would crash unexpectedly.

To avoid this type of error, validation could be used to check the data item before processing.

Presence Check Validation

Code is required to check if the user has input a value into a required field. If the data item is present it will pass the presence check. This is no guarantee that the data item is in an acceptable format and additional validation may be required.

Figure 8.02 shows a flowchart for a simple presence check on user input in which a textual value requires completion.

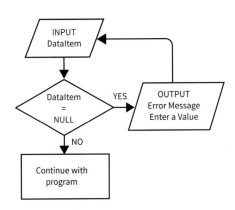

Figure 8.02 Presence Check flowchart

87

The process for dealing with presence checks in code differs between Console and Windows Forms applications.

In console mode a WHILE loop can be used to check the presence of the input. If the data is missing the user can be prompted again to enter the required data. This requires the Console.ReadLine method to pass the data before the check can be made.

```
Console.WriteLine("Insert Text Value")
    TextValue = Console.ReadLine
    Do While TextValue = ""
        Console.WriteLine("Please Input Text Value")
        TextValue = Console.ReadLine
    Loop
```

This method will work well with String data types but causes numeric data types to give an error. One solution is to make use of a temporary String variable to check the presence of the data before passing the data onto the numeric variable.

In Windows Forms applications the execution of code is triggered by an event such as a button press. The trigger cannot be controlled from within a WHILE loop in the same way as Console.ReadLine in console mode. A different approach is therefore needed.

The user is expected to input data prior to triggering the event and it is possible to check if the user input on the GUI has been completed. If the user input is missing the program can output an error message and end the subroutine, which forces the user to input data before re-triggering the event. If data is entered, it is passed to the variables.

For comparison with the Console Application code above, the following code uses a WHILE loop to implement such a check. If data is entered, the WHILE loop does not run and the data is passed to the variables. If data is not entered, the WHILE loop runs, outputs an error message and ends the subroutine; the last two lines are not executed so data is not passed to the variables.

```
Private Sub BTNInput _ Click (sender As Object, e As EventArgs) Handles BTNInput.Click

    Do While TBInputText.Text = "" Or TBInputInt.Text = ""
        MsgBox("A required field is empty")
        'The Exit Sub command stops the execution of the
        'subroutine, allowing the user to correct errors
        'before beginning the subroutine via Button on form
        Exit Sub
    Loop

    InputText = TBInputText.Text
    InputInt = TBInputInt.Text
```

However, this would not be a normal way to implement it – after all the WHILE loop can never run more than once. The following code uses an IF statement. If data is entered, the IF statement executes the ELSE branch and the data is passed to the variables. If data is not entered, the IF statement runs the THEN branch, outputs an error message and ends the subroutine.

```
Private Sub BTNInput _ Click (sender As Object, e As EventArgs) Handles BTNInput.Click

    If TBInputText.Text = "" Or TBInputInt.Text = "" Then
        MsgBox("A required field is empty")
        'The Exit Sub command stops the execution of the
        'subroutine, allowing the user to correct errors
        'before beginning the subroutine via Button on form
        Exit Sub
    Else
        InputText = TBInputText.Text
        InputInt = TBInputInt.Text
    End If
```

Range Check Validation

Figure 8.03 shows a flowchart and pseudocode for a range check used to ensure the day of the month entered by a user is in the range 1 to 31. The code could use a WHILE loop that checks the data against the required criteria. If the data input is acceptable the system will continue to run, if not the system will output an error message to the user.

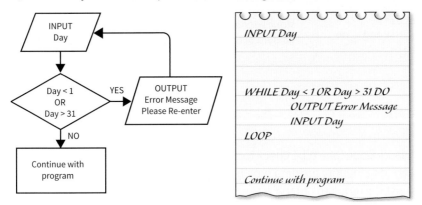

Figure 8.03 Flowchart and pseudocode for Range Check

```
Module Module1
    Dim Day As Integer
    Sub Main()
        Day = Console.ReadLine

        Do While Day < 1 Or Day > 31
            Console.WriteLine("Enter a
            value between 1 and 31")
            Day = Console.ReadLine
        Loop

        'program continues
    End Sub
End Module
```

TIP
WHILE loops check criteria before running. The criteria are defined to identify inputs outside of the required range. If acceptable values are input the loop never runs and the program continues. If inputs are outside of expected range the loops continues to iterate effectively halting the program until acceptable values are input.

Length Check Validation

Figure 8.04 shows a flowchart and pseudocode for a length check to ensure that a password consists of six or more characters. The code will need to calculate the length of the data item. It then follows a similar process to a range check using a WHILE loop to check the input against the required criteria. If the data input is acceptable the system will continue to run, if not the system will output an error message to the user.

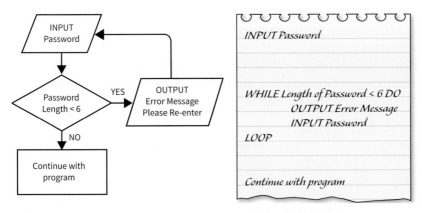

Figure 8.04 Flowchart and pseudocode for Length Check

```
Module Module1
    Dim Password As String
    Sub Main()

        Password = Console.ReadLine

        Do While Password.Length < 6
            Console.WriteLine("Password
            too short. Re-enter")
            Password = Console.ReadLine
        Loop

        'program continued
    End Sub
End Module
```

TIP

Note the use of the Length method to identify the number of characters in a string.

string variable.Length will return a integer value that represents the amount of characters (including spaces) in the string variable.

Type Check Validation

Figure 8.05 shows a flowchart and pseudocode for a type check to ensure that a number is entered as an integer. The code will need to identify the data type of the data item. It then uses a WHILE loop to check the input against the required criteria. If the data input is acceptable the system will continue to run, if not the system will output an error message to the user.

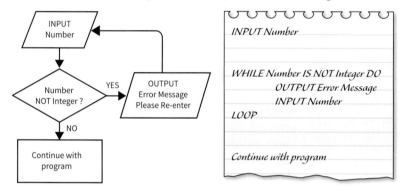

Figure 8.05 Flowchart and pseudocode for Type Check

While the pseudocode solution for type check validation is reasonably straightforward the code approach is more complex.

The IsNumeric function will check if a value is numeric. However it will accept non-integer numeric values.

```
Do While IsNumeric(TextValue) = False
    Console.WriteLine("Please Input a Number")
    TextValue = Console.ReadLine()
Loop
```

A more advanced approach is to use a series of pre-programmed, pre-tested code that has been made available to Visual Basic programmers to support these types of task. Figure 8.06 shows a WHILE loop condition that calls the TryParse function, a library routine which attempts to convert the input value into the data type indicated, in this case a 32-bit integer value. If successful the integer value is returned and the method is TRUE. If unsuccessful the value –1 is returned and the method is FALSE.

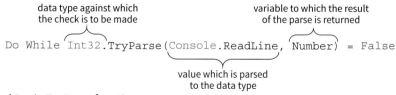

Figure 8.06 Visual Basic TryParse function

The following code makes use of the **TryParse** function:

```
Module Module1
    Dim Number As Integer
    Sub Main()

        Do While Int32.TryParse(Console.ReadLine, Number) = False
            Console.WriteLine("Error - Not Whole Number")
        Loop

        'program continues
    End Sub
```

Using **TryParse(...) = False** as the condition for the WHILE loop will cause the loop to continue while the conversion is unsuccessful. The loop will exit once a successful conversion has been made and the appropriate integer value has been returned to the variable **Number**.

Format Check Validation

Figure 8.07 shows a flowchart and pseudocode for a format check to ensure that a date is in the format dd/mm/yyyy. The code will be required to check each element of the data item to ensure it matches a predetermined pattern. If the data item matches the pattern the system will continue to run, if not the system will output an error message to the user.

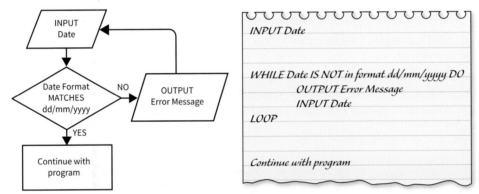

Figure 8.07 Flowchart and pseudocode for Format Check

As with the type check a series of pre-programmed Visual Basic library routines have been made available to programmers. The following example makes use of the **TryParse** method. It will not only validate incorrect date entries but also convert genuine dates to the date format.

```
Module Module1
    Dim Input As Date
    Sub Main()

        Do While Date.TryParse(Console.ReadLine, Input) = False
            Console.WriteLine("Date must be in format dd/mm/yyyy")
        Loop

        Console.WriteLine(Input)
        Console.ReadKey()

        'program continues
    End Sub
End Module
```

Using library routines does have dangers. Running the code with the input value 1/1/14 will produce an output of 01/01/2014, even though the user may have meant the year 1914. Inputting the full date 1/1/1914 avoids this error. It is possible to make use of the library routine `TryParseExact` but this is beyond the scope of this book. More information is available from the MSDN website at

https://msdn.microsoft.com/en-us/library/system.datetime.tryparseexact%28v=vs.110%29.aspx

Validation

1 Produce a flowchart and pseudocode for a system that will only accept positive numbers. Code a Console Application for this algorithm.

2 Produce a flowchart and pseudocode for a system that will only accept positive numbers less than 1000. Code a Console Application for this algorithm.

3 Code a Windows Forms Application for a system that will only accept positive numbers less than 1000.

4 Produce a flowchart and pseudocode for a system that will check that users have input a password that is longer than six characters. Code a program for this algorithm.

5 Program a function that will validate a user number and password from the user. All inputs must be validated against the following criteria:

- The user number must be a whole number in the range 1000 to 1500.

- The password must contain at least five characters.

The function will be passed the parameters of username and password and will return a Boolean value to indicate if the inputs match the validation criteria.

How would this code need to change if it was required to return a specific error message in addition to the Boolean value?

6 Produce a flowchart and pseudocode for a system that makes use of the function in Task 5. If the validation is completed successfully the system will output 'Welcome'. If the validation check is failed twice the system will output 'Locked Out' and exit the program.

Summary

- Accuracy of data entry is an important consideration in system design. Inaccurate data can lead to inaccurate outputs.

- Validation is a technique in which the system checks data input against a set of predetermined rules.

- Validation can identify obvious errors by detecting data that fails to meet the validation rules.

- Validation is able to ensure that data input is reasonable but cannot guarantee data accuracy.

- Five main forms of validation are used to check data as it is input:

  - Presence checks ensure that data has been input.

  - Range checks ensure that data falls within a predetermined range of values.

  - Length checks ensure that data inputs contains a predetermined number of characters.

  - Type checks ensure that data input is of a certain data type.

  - Format checks ensure that data input meets a predetermined format, such as dd/mm/yyyy.

- Verification checks the integrity of data when it is entered into the system. This is often completed by the individual inputting the data.

- Two common methods of verification are:

  - checking the input data against the original document or record

  - double entry in which the data is entered twice and the entries compared to identify differences.

Chapter 9:
Testing

9.01 Why Test Systems

In common with many products it is important to make sure systems work as expected before they are released to the final user. The complexity and critical nature of the system will determine the extent of the testing to be completed. It would be reasonable to expect that the computerised air traffic control system at an airport will have under gone extensive testing as failure could be catastrophic.

There are several notable examples of disasters caused by poor testing. The destruction of the unmanned Ariane 5 space rocket due to the failure of untested code sequences is one of the most costly with financial implications measured in billions of dollars. An article published in the New York Times magazine in December 1996 has more information about it (http://www.around.com/ariane.html).

9.02 When to Test

Testing can be broken into two distinct areas.

- **Alpha Testing** is completed during the programming of a system to check that the individual code sequences work as expected before they are combined to make the complete system. Testing during the programming stage can also be completed to help trace the source of unexpected outcomes.

- **Beta Testing** is formal testing once the system has been completed to ensure that the whole system meets expectations.

9.03 Debugging

Debugging is the process of detecting faults that cause errors in a program. This can be achieved by observing error messages produced by the IDE or by locating unexpected results. The types of error that can occur are divided into three groups.

Logical Errors

Logical errors are errors in the design of the program which allow the program to run but cause unexpected results. They can result from use of an incorrect formula or the incorrect use of control structures such as IF statements or loops. Examples include IF statements with incorrect conditions or loops that iterate the wrong number of times. Logical errors also derive from an incorrect sequence of statements, such as performing a calculation before assigning values to the variables.

Logical errors will probably not produce error messages as the code is running effectively. The problem is with the logic of the code not the execution of the code.

Syntax Errors

Syntax errors are errors in the use of the programming language such as incorrect punctuation or misspelling of variables and control words. Examples include IF statements with missing END IF or incorrect use of assignment. It is likely that the IDE will generate error messages indicating the reason for the error.

Runtime Errors

Runtime errors are errors that are only identified during the execution of the program. They can result from mismatched data types, overflow or divide-by-zero operations.

Data type errors include:

- passing string data to an integer variable, which will probably cause the system to crash

- passing real data to an integer variable; the variable will round the input data to the nearest whole number – the system will execute the code but produce unexpected results.

Overflow errors occur when the data passed to a variable is too large to be held by the data type selected. In the theory element of the IGCSE you will have used this term to describe a situation where a 9-bit binary number is stored in an 8-bit byte. This can often result from calculations during the execution of a program. For example, the data type Short can be used to hold numbers between –32 767 and +32 767. If a variable of this data type was assigned the result of the square of any number greater than 182, it would produce an overflow error.

In mathematics it is not possible to divide by zero because any number can be divided by zero an infinite number of times. If a program includes a division calculation that divides by a variable holding the value zero, the system will produce a divide-by-zero error.

SYLLABUS CHECK

Problem-solving and design: identify errors in given algorithms and suggest ways of removing these errors.

9.04 IDE Debugging Tools and Diagnostics

Many IDEs include sophisticated diagnostics designed to identify possible bugs and provide the user with supportive error messages. Of course these tools are only able to identify errors in the code not in the logic of the code and as a result are unable to identify logical errors. Visual Studio Express provides debugging support for both syntax and runtime errors.

Syntax Diagnostics

Syntax errors are identified and underlined during the process of typing the code. Supporting error messages are available when the cursor is placed over the underlined code. An error window also provides information about errors including the line number of the error.

Figure 9.01 shows two types of syntax error message in the code creation window.

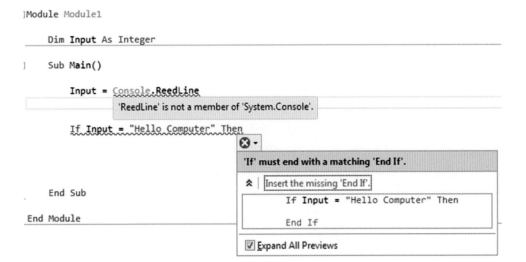

Figure 9.01 Error message detail window

In the first instance a control word, 'Readline' is incorrectly spelt – 'Reedline' cannot be identified by the IDE. The second error message indicates that the IF statement has not been correctly terminated. The same information is also held in the error list. To show the error list use the drop-down option from the VIEW tab (Figure 9.02).

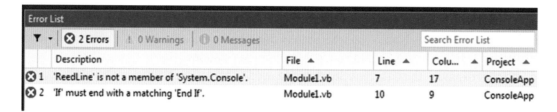

Figure 9.02 Visual Studio Error List window

Runtime Diagnostics

Runtime errors are detected during execution of a program and specific error messages are provided. In Figure 9.01 the user has declared Input as an Integer variable although would appear to expect textual input from the user. The IDE cannot detected that error – it would only occur at runtime (see Figure 9.03).

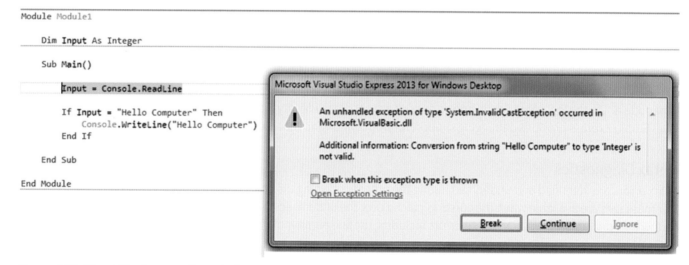

Figure 9.03 Visual Studio exception window

9.05 Identifying Logical Errors

While the IDE is able to support programmers with syntax and runtime errors it cannot identify logical errors. The system will operate and process data by following the code that has been written – it is unable to determine if the code contains logical errors that result in unexpected outputs.

The process of identifying logical errors has to be part of the testing process. When unexpected outputs are recognised it is likely that a logical error will be present in the code. The actual error will also have to be identified manually.

9.06 Dry Running

Dry running is the process of working through a section of code manually to locate logical or runtime errors. This type of testing is often documented in a trace table which will identify the changes in values within a system during its operation. The values traced could relate to the inputs, outputs or variables used in the process. It would be usual to use a table that shows the variables as columns with the changing values during execution being recorded in rows in chronological order.

Tracing Pseudocode

The following pseudocode algorithm is intended to calculate the quotient division of X by Y.

```
INT: X ← 0, Y ← 0, W ← 0
INPUT X, Y
WHILE X > Y
    X ← X - Y
    W ← W + 1
LOOP
OUTPUT W
```

Complete the trace table (Table 9.01) when the input values are X = 50 and Y = 15.

The comments have been added to help explain the trace table and are not normally required in a formal trace table.

Table 9.01

X	Y	W	Output	Comments
0	0	0		Initialisation values of the variables.
50	15	0		The new values are input.
35	15	1		X is reduced by 15, W is incremented by 1. Loop returns to the WHILE condition check. As X > Y, loop runs.
20	15	2		X is reduced by 15, W is incremented by 1. Loop returns to the WHILE condition check. As X > Y, loop runs.
5	15	3		X is reduced by 15, W is incremented by 1. Loop returns to the WHILE condition check. As X < Y, loop exits.
			3	The value in W is output.

EXTENSION TASK

Trace Table

The pseudocode algorithm contains a logical error. Complete a trace table with the input values of X = 60 and Y = 15 to identify the error.

Tracing a Flowchart

Study the flowchart in Figure 9.04.

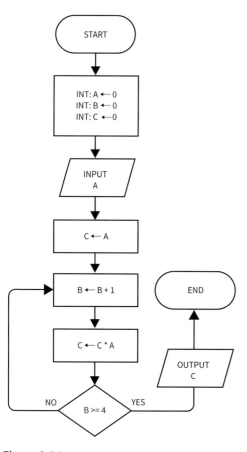

Figure 9.04

Table 9.02

A	B	C	Output	Comments
0	0	0		Initialised values
2	0	0		Input A
2	1	2		C ← A B ← B + 1
2	1	4		C ← C * A Will loop as B < 4
2	2	8		B ← B + 1 C ← C * A Will loop as B < 4
2	3	16		B ← B + 1 C ← C * A Will loop as B < 4
2	4	32		B ← B + 1 C ← C * A Loop exited as B = 4
2	4	32	32	Output value in C

Complete a trace table where the input value is A = 2 (see Table 9.02).

TASK

Discussion Question

What is the aim of this program?

9.07 Breakpoints, Variable Tracing and Stepping Through Code

Although the IDE cannot identify logical errors it does provide tools that assist the programmer in the manual process of error identification. Visual Studio Express, in common with many IDEs, provides the programmer with the ability to execute the program one line at a time, displaying the values held in variables when the cursor hovers over them. To allow the programmer to check particular segments of code the system can be set to execute as normal until it meets a 'breakpoint' created by the programmer at which time it will run in single-line execution mode.

The following algorithm has been designed to calculate the number of tins of paint required to cover a wall. The user inputs the length and height of the wall in metres and also the area that can be covered by one tin of paint. The algorithm does not produce the expected results.

```
Module Module1

    Dim Length, Height As Decimal
    Dim Area, Cover As Decimal
    Dim Tins As Integer

    Sub Main()

        Console.WriteLine("Input Length in Metres")
        Length = Console.ReadLine
        Console.WriteLine("Input Height in Metres")
        Height = Console.ReadLine
        Console.WriteLine("How many square metres covered by 1 tin?")
        Cover = Console.ReadLine

        Area = Length + Height

        Tins = Area / Cover

        Console.WriteLine(Tins)

        Console.ReadKey()

    End Sub
End Module
```

The programmer decides to use the breakpoint diagnostic tool to help identify the error. The breakpoint is to be inserted after the input sequence as the programmer is happy that the correct inputs are being obtained. To test the system the programmer decides to use a length of 5 metres and a height of 2 metres; the expected area is 10 square metres.

To insert the breakpoint, right click at the desired line of code and select Breakpoint – Insert Breakpoint from the menu (see Figure 9.05).

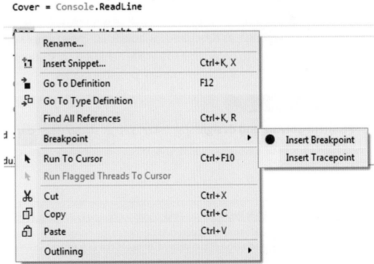

Figure 9.05 Breakpoint insert menu

The breakpoint will be indicated by brown highlighting (Figure 9.06). To delete or disable the breakpoint right click the red point indicator to the left of the line numbers

Figure 9.06 Visual Basic code showing a breakpoint

When the code is run it will execute as normal until the breakpoint is reached. To step into the code click the step tool button (Figure 9.07) or press F11. These tools will only become available when a breakpoint has been activated.

Figure 9.07 Breakpoint Step Tool

The line of code being executed will be highlighted in yellow (see Figure 9.08). Hovering over the variables will show the value currently contained. You will have to click on the code window to select it before you can trace the variable.

In Figure 9.08, the area is 7 not the expected 10, leading the programmer to identify an error in the calculation of area. They have incorrectly used addition (5 + 2 = 7), not the expected multiplication (5 * 2 = 10).

Figure 9.08 Displaying contents of a variable

TASK

Breakpoint

Once this error was fixed the programmer continued to receive unexpected outputs for some test values.

1 Write the program and, using breakpoints and a range of data, identify the remaining error.

2 Decide how you might correct this error.

9.08 Beta Testing

A formal test schedule is designed to test all possible events that a system could experience. It will test normal expected operation as well as extreme inputs or usage. The test schedule will identify the elements of the system to be tested and the data to be used in the tests. Each set of test data and the expected outcome is known as a 'test case'. The data used will fall into three categories, as described in Table 9.03. The example data in Table 9.03 is based on a system designed to determine the grade achieved by students in an examination, with inputs of student marks and the maximum possible marks.

SYLLABUS CHECK

Problem-solving and design: suggest and apply suitable test data.

Table 9.03

Type of test	Description	Example data
Valid data	Data that is expected to be met in the normal operation of the system. It meets the expected validation rules. The system should produce the expected outcome.	Integer values between zero and the maximum possible score.
Invalid data (also known as 'erroneous data')	Data that would not form part of the expected input range. The system should reject the data and output appropriate error messages.	Non-integer values (it is not possible to get half a mark). Values less than zero or more than the maximum score. Textual inputs, such as 'TEN'.
Boundary data	Data that is at the boundary of the criteria that determine the path of execution of code.	Data that falls at grade boundaries. The grade boundary for an A is 80% and the maximum mark is 100. Data one mark below the grade boundary: 79. Data one mark above the grade boundary: 81.

Beta Testing

Amongst other data a system holds the mobile telephone number and age next birthday of current patients in a hospital. Mobile telephone numbers are entered as NNNNN-NNNNNN where N is a number. For each of the data items, decide on:

1 the appropriate data type

2 appropriate validation that could be applied

3 invalid and, where appropriate, boundary data that could be used to test input validation.

9.09 Testing Tasks

Task 1

Study the flowchart in Figure 9.09.

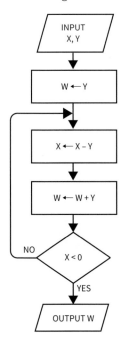

Create a trace table showing the values of the variables X, Y and W during execution of the algorithm and the OUTPUT for input values of:

1 X = 16 and Y = 7

2 X = 10 and Y = 5

Figure 9.09

Task 2

The following algorithm, designed to calculate the factorial of a number, contains a number of logical errors. Identify the errors **and** explain how they could be corrected. You may like to use a trace table to help identify the errors.

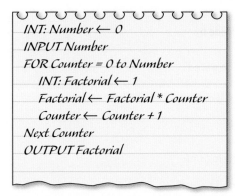

```
INT: Number ← 0
INPUT Number
FOR Counter = 0 to Number
    INT: Factorial ← 1
    Factorial ← Factorial * Counter
    Counter ← Counter + 1
Next Counter
OUTPUT Factorial
```

SYLLABUS CHECK

Problem-solving and design: identify errors in given algorithms and suggest ways of removing these errors.

Task 3

The following algorithm is designed to accept a series of numbers with the sequence being ended by the user inputting a negative number. At the end of the sequence the system will output the smallest number input and the sum of the numbers input. The algorithm contains a number of logical errors. Identify the errors **and** explain how they could be corrected.

> **TIP**
> There are five different logical errors.

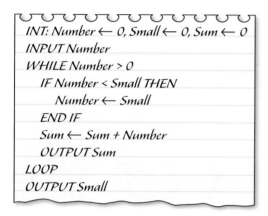

```
INT: Number ← 0, Small ← 0, Sum ← 0
INPUT Number
WHILE Number > 0
    IF Number < Small THEN
        Number ← Small
    END IF
    Sum ← Sum + Number
    OUTPUT Sum
LOOP
OUTPUT Small
```

Task 4

A local athletics club holds the following data about individual athletes:

- height (in metres)
- ID (a five-digit membership identification number)
- surname.

For each of the data items, identify:

1 the appropriate data type
2 an appropriate validation check
3 invalid and, where appropriate, boundary data that could be used to test the validation.

Summary

- It is important to test systems to ensure they will perform as expected.
- Logical errors are errors in the logic of the process performed by the code. The code will run but will produce unexpected results.
- Syntax errors are errors in the syntax used within the code. It is likely that these will be identified by the IDE diagnostics.
- Runtime errors only become apparent during the execution of the code. Attempting to divide by zero is a common runtime error.
- Trace tables provide a structure by which the value of variables, inputs and outputs can be traced at each step of an algorithm. They can be helpful in identifying logical errors.
- Valid data is data met by the system in its normal operation.
- Invalid data is data that the system is not expecting. It should identify and reject the data providing appropriate error messages.
- Boundary data is data that falls at the boundaries of value changes. It is used to check the logic of the comparisons used to determine those value changes.

Chapter 10:
Arrays

Learning objectives

By the end of this chapter you will understand:

- how to define an array using flowcharts and pseudocode
- how to declare and use an array
- how to read and write values from an array
- how you can use a number of arrays to organise data.

10.01 What Is an Array?

An **array** is a data structure that can hold a set of data items under a single identifier. In the same way that a variable holds data of a specific data type and has a name that can be used to identify it, an array also holds data of a specific type and can be referred to by its name or label. The major difference is that while a variable can only hold one data value an array can hold multiple values. For example if you wished to store the surnames of 25 students using variables you would have to declare 25 variables. Using an array you could store all 25 values in a single array set up to accept 25 data items.

KEY TERM

Array: A variable that can hold a set of data items of the same data type under a single identifier.

10.02 Declaring an Array

Declaring an array is a similar process to declaring a variable; the same naming and data type requirements exist. The difference is that you need to define the size of the array which will be determined by the number of data items that the array is required to hold. Each individual value held within an array is identified by an index number. Index numbers are sequential and in Visual Basic the numbering starts from zero.

Table 10.01 is a diagrammatic representation of an array designed to hold the first five letters of the Greek alphabet.

Table 10.01

Index number	0	1	2	3	4
Data item	Alpha	Beta	Gamma	Delta	Epsilon

The pseudocode format for declaring an array capable of holding the five values is as follows. Note how the range of indices is 0 to 4:

```
STRING: GreekLetter [0:4]
```

Not all languages number array items from zero and you may see an example of arrays that start from 1. In this example the final index would then become 5:

```
STRING: GreekLetter [1:5]
```

When writing pseudocode either method of numbering is acceptable, but it is vital to remain consistent when using arrays in algorithms. If the array is declared as [0:4] then the following pseudocode must also follow that format with the last data item being held in index 4.

SYLLABUS CHECK

Data structures: declare the size of one-dimensional arrays.

The syntax for declaring an array in Visual Basic is shown in Figure 10.01.

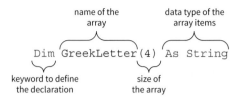

Figure 10.01 Visual Basic array declaration syntax

In Visual Basic the size of the array is defined by stating the final index number. The first index position of zero is assumed. The range of this array is [0:4], representing five individually numbered items.

10.03 Initialising Arrays

While it is common to initialise a variable it is unusual to initialise an array unless you want to place specific data items in the array at the time of declaration. If you wish to initialise an array in Visual Basic the size of the array is defined by the number of data items used to initialise the array. The explicit reference to size has to be omitted from the ( ) by removing the number:

```
Dim GreekLetter() As String = {"Alpha", "Beta", "Gamma", "Delta", "Epsilon"}
```

10.04 Using Arrays

Arrays offer programmers advantages over variables. As we have seen they allow many data items to be stored under a single identifier. They give the programmer the ability to reference any individual data item by the appropriate **array index** and to use iteration to complete read, write or search operations by looping through the data items. This makes arrays particularly effective when working with data records.

KEY TERM

Array index: a sequential number that references the items of an array.

SYLLABUS CHECK

Data structures: show understanding of the use of a variable as an index of an array.

Reading and Writing Data Items

To read a data item you reference it by the array name and the index number. For example, `GreekLetter(2)` holds the data item 'Gamma'. The same logic applies when writing values to an array. The following code would write the letter 'C' to the item at the specified index position replacing the original data item:

```
GreekLetter(2) = "C"
```

Declare an array named 'Task' that is capable of holding four integer values. Write code to allow the user to input a data item to selected array positions. Write code to allow the user to output the value held in a selected array position.

Figure 10.02(a) shows the flowchart for the input process and Figure 10.02(b) shows the flowchart for the output process. Figure 10.03 shows the corresponding pseudocode for the processes.

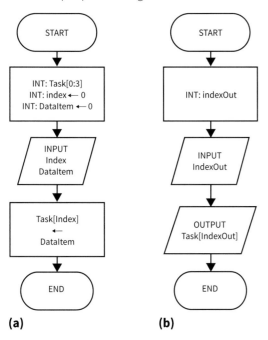

(a)   **(b)**

Figure 10.02 Array Input and Output flowchart

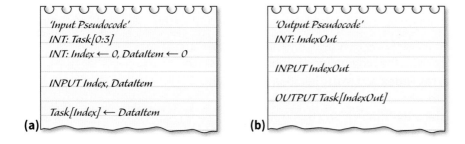

(a)   **(b)**

Figure 10.03 Array Input and Output pseudocode

A Windows Forms Application could be used to produce the system. The interface could be designed as shown in Figure 10.04 with a button to run the subroutines for each of the input and output processes. Textboxes accept the input and display the output.

Figure 10.04 Windows Forms interface design

The names of the textboxes used in the example code are shown in green. The code required to produce the system would be as follows:

```
Public Class Form1
    'Global declaration of the array to give scope to both subroutines
    Dim Task(3) As Integer

    Private Sub BTNInput _ Click(sender As Object, e As EventArgs) Handles BTNInput.Click
        'Local declaration and initialisation of Input variables
        Dim Index As Integer = 0
        Dim DataItem As Integer = 0

        'Obtaining user input
        Index = TBIndex.Text
        DataItem = TBDataItem.Text

        'Input of DataItem into selected index
        Task(Index) = DataItem

    End Sub

    Private Sub BTNOutput _ Click(sender As Object, e As EventArgs) Handles BTNOutput.Click
        'Local declaration and initialisation of Output variable
        Dim IndexOut As Integer = 0

        'Obtaining user selection of index to display
        IndexOut = TBIndexOut.Text

        'Displaying the data item at the selected index in the Textbox
        TBDisplay.Text = Task(IndexOut)

    End Sub
End Class
```

EXTENSION TASK

Reading from and Writing to an Array

Try to write or read data with index 4. Try to input a textual value into the array. Both these actions will cause the system to crash and output an error message.

1 Consider appropriate validation methods that could be used to prevent the user entering the types of invalid data above.

2 Draw a flowchart and create a pseudocode algorithm that includes these validation techniques.

3 Test that your algorithms work by programming and running the code in Visual Basic and using suitable test data.

Iteration in Arrays

The process of reading individual array positions can be extended by using iteration to read all the positions in an array. This allows iterative code to be used to check multiple data values.

Where the size of the array is known, a FOR loop can achieve the required iterative process. The counter variable in the FOR loop can be used to iterate through the index positions.

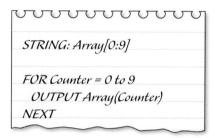

Data structures: read or write values in an array using a FOR..TO..NEXT loop.

The following pseudocode shows how iteration can be used to output all the data items in a ten-item array:

```
STRING: Array[0:9]

FOR Counter = 0 to 9
   OUTPUT Array(Counter)
NEXT
```

Declare an array called Letters that is capable of holding six single characters. Initialise the array with letters A to F. Write code that allows the user to input a letter and then search the array to identify if the letter input is in the array.

Figure 10.05 shows a flowchart and pseudocode for the algorithm.

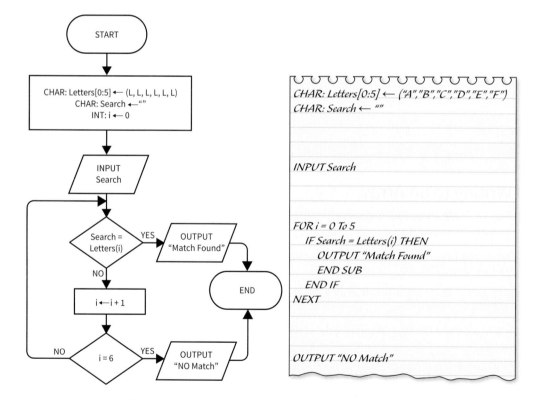

Figure 10.05 Flowchart and pseudocode for search algorithm

The FOR loop condition has been set to follow the declaration of the array, which has an index from 0 to 5. Once a match has been found the subroutine is ended. The 'NO Match' message is only shown if the loop has completed.

The following coded solution uses console mode:

```
Module Module1
    'Global declaration of the array
    Dim Letters() As Char = {"A", "B", "C", "D", "E", "F"}

    'Main set to allow iterative calling of the Search subroutine
    'while 1 is selected by user
    Sub Main()
        Dim Action As String = "1"

        Do While Action = 1

            Call Search()

            Console.WriteLine("Continue to Search Array ?")
            Console.WriteLine("Enter 1 to continue OR any other number to exit")
            Action = Console.ReadLine
        Loop
    End Sub

    'Subroutine to search the array
    Sub Search()
        Dim Search As Char = ""
        Console.WriteLine("Enter character for search")
        Search = Console.ReadLine

        'FOR loop iterates through all positions in the array
        'at each iteration the value of i increments and the index position searched
        'also increments in line with the changes in the value of i
        For i = 0 To Letters.Length - 1
            If Search = Letters(i) Then
                Console.WriteLine("Match Found")
                Console.ReadKey()
                'Exit Sub used to stop subroutine once a match is found
                Exit Sub
            End If
        Next

        Console.WriteLine("NO Match")
        Console.ReadKey()
    End Sub
End Module
```

TIP
Notice the use of .Length to identify the number of indexes in the array Letters. Because arrays are numbered from zero it is important to subtract one to represent the number of the final index.

EXTENSION TASK

Using iteration with an Array

The current system will stop once a match is found. This would be an ideal situation if the values are all unique but this may not be the case.

1 Draw a flowchart and create a pseudocode algorithm for a Search subroutine that searches the entire array to check for multiple matches. The output should be the number of occasions a match was found.

2 Test that your algorithm works by programming and running the code in Visual Basic.

10.05 Groups of Arrays

If you need to hold multiple data elements for each data record it is possible to use arrays in groups. Provided the same index number is used in each array for the data items that relate to one record the values of multiple data items can be read.

Consider a situation where a system holds the records shown in Table 10.02.

Table 10.02

Student ID	Surname	Computing Grade
1001	Morgan	A
1002	Smith	C
1003	Jones	B

These data items could be held in three arrays as shown in Tables 10.03, 10.04 and 10.05 with the same index position in each array referring to the data regarding one record. As ID 1002 is held at index position 1 in the ID array, the remaining data for that record is held in index position 1 in the other two arrays.

Table 10.03 ID array

Index	0	1	2
Data Item	1001	1002	1003

Table 10.04 Surname array

Index	0	1	2
Data Item	Morgan	Smith	Jones

Table 10.05 Grade array

Index	0	1	2
Data Item	A	C	B

The pseudocode to output the Surname and Grade for a given student ID would be as follows:

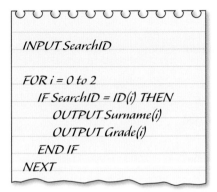

```
INPUT SearchID

FOR i = 0 to 2
    IF SearchID = ID(i) THEN
        OUTPUT Surname(i)
        OUTPUT Grade(i)
    END IF
NEXT
```

10.06 Array Tasks

Task 1

1   Draw a flowchart and create a pseudocode algorithm that iterates through an array of integers and outputs the average. Declare and initialise the array with the following set of integers: 12, 14, 10, 6, 7, 11 and 3.

2   Test that your algorithm works by programming and running the code in Visual Basic.

Task 2

An algorithm will take an integer value, n. It will call a subroutine to place into an array 12 incremental multiples of n (the first array index will hold $1 \times n$ and the last index position $12 \times n$). An additional subroutine will allow the user to output all the multiples in order.

1   Draw a flowchart and create pseudocode for this algorithm.

2   Test that your algorithm works by programming and running the code in Visual Basic.

Task 3

The data in Table 10.06 is to be organised in arrays so that the user can search via User ID and the system will display all the data related to that User ID.

Table 10.06

User ID	Age	Gender
112	45	Male
217	16	Female
126	27	Female

1   Draw a flowchart and create a pseudocode algorithm that accepts a User ID and displays the related data.

2   Test that your algorithm works by programming and running the code in Visual Basic.

Summary

- An array is a variable that can hold a set of data items, of the same data type, under a single identifier.

- When an array is declared, its size is defined. Visual Basic numbers elements in an array from zero.

- Each element or data item in an array can be referenced by its index.

- The index can be used to read or write values in an array.

- A FOR loop can be used to iterate through the index locations in an array. The loop counter is used to identify successive index numbers.

- Holding records which consist of more than one data item can be achieved by the use of multiple arrays. Data for each record is held at the same index position in the different arrays.

Chapter 11:
Directional Instructions

Learning objectives

By the end of this chapter you will understand:

■ the use of the Logo language used with floor turtles

■ how to describe the path of a floor turtle as a sequence of instructions

■ how to use REPEAT..ENDREPEAT to iterate a sequence of instructions.

11.01 Floor Turtle Instructions

You can be asked to write a series of logical steps to complete a task, which will often make use of a floor turtle. A turtle is a robot (see Figure 11.01) that can be programmed to draw a line by following a path and placing a pen on the floor to create the line.

The language that is used to control the robot consists of simple directional commands and is based on the Logo programming language. There are many online sites and applications that allow users to control an onscreen turtle by use of a Logo instruction program. The language and syntax of these applications has developed a long way from the early Logo language with some providing multiple turtles and complex 3D graphics.

Figure 11.01 Floor Turtle

A common instruction set for a floor turtle is shown in Table 11.01.

Table 11.01

Instruction	Meaning
FORWARD *d*	Move *d* cm forward
BACKWARD *d*	Move *d* cm backward
LEFT *t*	Turn left *t* degrees
RIGHT *t*	Turn right *t* degrees
REPEAT *n*	Repeat the next set of instructions *n* times
ENDREPEAT	End of the REPEAT loop
PENUP	Raise the pen (stop drawing)
PENDOWN	Lower the pen (start drawing)

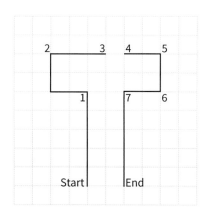

Figure 11.02 Shape defined by instructions in Table 11.02

Each square in Figure 11.02 is 20 pixels by 20 pixels. Beginning at the start point, complete the set of instructions to draw the incomplete T shape.

TIP

Instructions are written from the perspective of the turtle. It can help to imagine that you are walking the floor and drawing the line. The instructions are the turns and steps you would have to take to complete the drawing.

Assume that the turtle is at the start point, with the drawing pen up and facing up the page. It is usual to be given the beginning state of the pen in a task description.

Table 11.02 shows the instructions to draw the shape in Figure 11.02. The comments are to help understanding and would not be required in an answer to a question. The numbers are included in Figure 11.02 to refer to the position in the drawing that has been reached.

There is no need to include the measurement of distance. The instruction FORWARD 100 is correct; it is not required to read FORWARD 100 pixels.

Table 11.02

Instruction number	Instruction	Comments
1	PENDOWN	The turtle lowers the pen to start drawing.
2	FORWARD 100	The turtle moves forward 100 pixels – five squares each of 20 pixels in length. It is now at positon 1.
3	LEFT 90	The turtle turns 90 degrees left and is now facing left. Although not as logical, a right turn of 270 degrees (RIGHT 270) would have the same effect.
4	FORWARD 40	The turtle moves forward 40 pixels.
5	RIGHT 90	The turtle turns 90 degrees right to face up.
6	FORWARD 40	The turtle moves forward 40 pixels. It is now at position 2.
7	RIGHT 90	The turtle turns 90 degrees right to face right.
8	FORWARD 60	The turtle moves forward 60 pixels to position 3.
9	PENUP	The turtle raises the pen.
10	FORWARD 20	The turtle moves forward 20 pixels without leaving a line. It is now at position 4.
11	PENDOWN	The turtle lowers the pen to start drawing again.
12	FORWARD 40	The turtle moves forward 40 pixels to position 5.
13	RIGHT 90	The turtle turns 90 degrees right to face down the page.
14	FORWARD 40	The turtle moves forward 40 pixels to positon 6.
15	RIGHT 90	The turtle turns 90 degrees right to face left across the page.
16	FORWARD 40	The turtle moves forward 40 pixels to position 7.
17	LEFT 90	The turtle turns 90 degrees left to face down the page.
18	FORWARD 100	The turtle moves forward 100 pixels to the End position.

A valid alternative to instructions 13, 14 and 15 would have been:

13 LEFT 90 – Turn to face up the page

14 BACKWARD 40 – Move backwards down the page

15 LEFT 90 – Turn to face left across the page

11.02 Iteration in the Instructions

In common with other programming languages it would be normal to use iteration to avoid repeating code. In the context of a floor turtle this situation can be identified where a sequence of moves repeats.

The only loop that is possible is a REPEAT(N)..ENDREPEAT structure. The number of iterations is indicated as the parameter value, N. ENDREPEAT indicates the end of the looped section of code and returns execution to the REPEAT until all required iterations have been completed.

TIP

A common error when designing the instructions to perform iterations is to miss out the ENDREPEAT statement. This is a syntax error and would cause program errors.

> **1** Where would it be possible to use a REPEAT..ENDREPEAT in these instructions?
>
> **2** How would you write the new REPEAT..ENDREPEAT instruction?

11.03 Floor Turtle Tasks

Task 1

Each square on Figure 11.03 is 10 pixels by 10 pixels. The turtle is at the start point, with the drawing pen up and facing up the page.

Complete the instructions to draw the shape.

1 LEFT 90

2 PENDOWN

Make use of the REPEAT instruction.

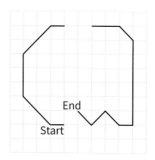

Figure 11.03

Task 2

Each square on Figure 11.04 is 20 pixels by 20 pixels. The diagonal distance across each square is 28 pixels. The turtle is at the start point, with the drawing pen up and facing up the page. Write the instructions to draw the shape.

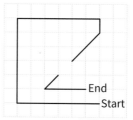

Figure 11.04

Task 3

Each square on Figure 11.05 is 20 pixels by 20 pixels. The diagonal distance across each square is 28 pixels. The turtle is at the start point, with the drawing pen up and facing up the page.

1 LEFT 90

2 PENDOWN

3 REPEAT

Figure 11.05 Complete the instructions to draw the shape.

Summary

- A floor turtle makes use of sequences of directional and movement-based instructions.

- The instruction set makes use of sequence and iteration statements to describe the path that the turtle is to follow.

12 Examination Practice

This is a series of examination-style questions. At the end of the chapter there is a mark scheme for exam-style questions which provides examples of correct solutions. It also indicates how the marks might be awarded for programming questions, where there is often more than one correct solution.

12.01 Questions

1 Consider the following algorithm:

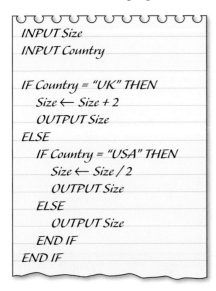

```
INPUT Size
INPUT Country

IF Country = "UK" THEN
    Size ← Size + 2
    OUTPUT Size
ELSE
    IF Country = "USA" THEN
        Size ← Size / 2
        OUTPUT Size
    ELSE
        OUTPUT Size
    END IF
END IF
```

What size will be output for the following inputs?

Size	Country	Output
20	USA	
19	France	
14	UK	

[3]

2 This section of pseudocode loops through an array called NUM which already holds 50 positive numbers. The index of the first number is index 1. The code will output the smallest number.

```
Small ← 0
FOR Counter = 1 To 50
    IF NUM(Counter) < Small THEN
        NUM(Counter) ← Small
    END IF
    Counter ← Counter + 1
    OUTPUT Small
NEXT
```

There are four errors in this code.

Locate these errors and suggest a corrective piece of code. [8]

3   The following pseudocode inputs the time taken to complete a 100-metre sprint.
A value of –1 stops the input. The information output is the average time taken
and the number of runs that took 20 or more seconds.

```
Count ← 0
Number ← 0
Total ← 0
Time ← 0

INPUT Time
WHILE Time > 0
    Total ← Total + Time
    IF Time >= 20 THEN
        Number ← Number + 1
    END IF
    Count ← Count + 1
    INPUT Time
LOOP
Average ← Total/Count
OUPUT Average, Number
```

Complete the trace table for the following sequence of input values: 18, 19, 24, 21,
18, 17, 23, 20, 19, 21, –1.

Time	Total	Number	Count	Average	Output

[6]

4   Write an algorithm using pseudocode or a flowchart only, which inputs three integers
N1, N2 and N3 and outputs the smallest of the three numbers.   [3]

5   One type of validation is a presence check. Suggest other validation techniques that could be used for the following data inputs. For each technique give an example of invalid data that could be used to test the validation rule.

Data input	Validation technique	Invalid test data
Mobile phone number		
Height of a person		
Number of brothers		

[6]

6   The flowchart inputs a sequence of numbers: a value below zero stops the input.

Complete the trace table for the input data: 11, 9, –2

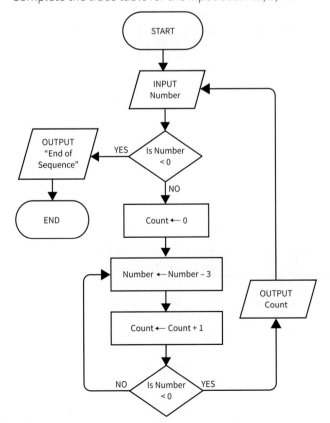

Number	Count	Output

[4]

7 A floor turtle uses these instructions:

Instruction	Meaning
FORWARD *d*	Move *d* cm forward
BACKWARD *d*	Move *d* cm backward
LEFT *t*	Turn left *t* degrees
RIGHT *t*	Turn right *t* degrees

Instruction	Meaning
REPEAT *n*	Repeat the next set of Instructions *n* times
ENDREPEAT	End of the REPEAT loop
PENUP	Raise the pen (stop drawing)
PENDOWN	Lower the pen (start drawing)

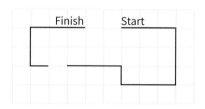

Each square in the drawing is 10 cm by 10 cm.

Complete the set of instructions to draw the shape (shown in bold lines).

> PENDOWN
>
> RIGHT 90
>
> REPEAT 3
>
> ....

[4]

8 The flowchart shows the system used at a set of automatic crossing gates on a junction of a railway and a road. The system constantly checks for a signal sent from an approaching train. When the signal is received the system activates warning lights and, after a period of time, closes the gates unless traffic is on the crossing. When the crossing gates are closed the train is sent an approach signal. The system will open the gates once the train has passed unless another train is approaching.

Complete the flowchart using the following instructions. **Only use** the instruction numbers to complete the flowchart.

Instruction number	Instruction
1	Has Train Passed?
2	Wait 15 Seconds
3	Warning Lights OFF
4	Warning Lights ON
5	Gates CLOSE
6	Crossing Clear?
7	Signal Received?

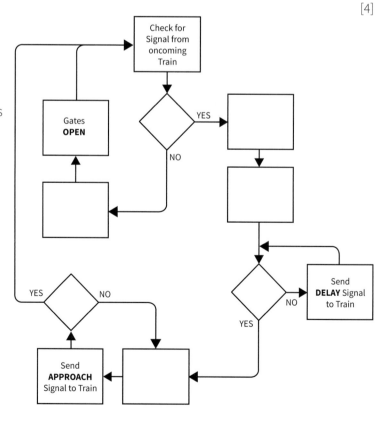

[4]

9 The following data about a group of students is to be stored in three arrays:

NAME[1:6]

ID[1:6]

SCORE[1:6]

Name	ID	Score
David	D167	120
Alan	A447	96
Manjit	M892	112
Jatinder	J098	100
Barrac	B492	99
Taona	T873	103

Write an algorithm using pseudocode which:

- inputs a target score
- outputs the Name and ID of all students who have a score higher than that target score. [3]

10 Abdulla requires a system to check if a four-digit number meets the following rules:

- The sum of the digits must not be a multiple of 5.
- The sum of the first two digits must not be less than the sum of the last two digits.

For example:

- 6423 is invalid because $6 + 4 + 2 + 3 = 15$ which is a multiple of 5.
- 3256 is invalid because $3 + 2$ is less than $5 + 6$.

Write an algorithm using pseudocode or a flowchart which takes four single digits as input and outputs "VALID" or "INVALID" to indicate if the input meets the above rules [5]

13 Solutions

Chapter 3 Variables and Arithmetic Operators

Multiply Machine Extension Task

Figure 13.01 shows an example of the interface that could be used with this task.

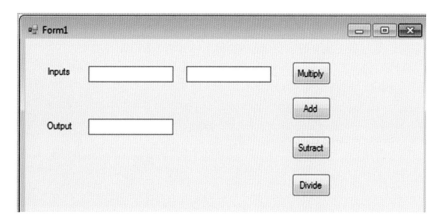

Figure 13.01 Windows Forms interface for Multiply Machine

```
Public Class Form1

    'Global declaration of inputs to allow all routines access
    Dim Number1 As Integer = 0
    Dim Number2 As Integer = 0

    Private Sub BTNMultiply_Click(sender As Object, e As EventArgs) Handles BTNMultiply.Click

        'Declaration of required local variable
        Dim Multi As Integer = 0

        'Storing the values input in the textboxes to the variables
        Number1 = TBNumber1.Text
        Number2 = TBNumber2.Text

        'Storing in the local variable the multiplication
        Multi = Number1 * Number2

        'Displaying the value held in the variable Multi in the output text box
        TBOutput.Text = Multi

    End Sub

    Private Sub BTNAdd_Click(sender As Object, e As EventArgs) Handles BTNAdd.Click
        'Declaration of required local variable
        Dim Add As Integer = 0

        Number1 = TBNumber1.Text
        Number2 = TBNumber2.Text

        'Storing in the local variable the addition
        Add = Number1 + Number2

        TBOutput.Text = Add
    End Sub
```

```vbnet
Private Sub BTNSubtract _ Click(sender As Object, e As EventArgs) Handles BTNSubtract.Click
    'Declaration of required local variable
    Dim Subtract As Integer = 0

    Number1 = TBNumber1.Text
    Number2 = TBNumber2.Text

    'Storing in the local variable the subtraction
    Subtract = Number1 - Number2

        TBOutput.Text = Subtract
End Sub

Private Sub BTNDivide _ Click(sender As Object, e As EventArgs) Handles BTNDivide.Click
    'Declaration of required local variable
    'Data Type of Decimal because division of Integers can result in a decimal
    Dim Divide As Decimal = 0

    Number1 = TBNumber1.Text
    Number2 = TBNumber2.Text

    'Storing in the local variable the division
    Divide = Number1 / Number2

    TBOutput.Text = Divide
End Sub

End Class
```

Points for discussion:

1 It would be useful to declare the variables holding the input values as global variables so they can be accessed by all the subroutines. It would also be possible to declare the result as a global variable and allow each routine to change its value depending on the aim of the routine.

2 As the inputs are integers the multiply, addition and subtract operation will all produce an integer value result. The divide operation could however produce a decimal value (consider 10 divided by 3) and the result would therefore need to be held as a Decimal or Single data type. If the divide result was stored as an Integer value it would be rounded to the nearest whole number.

Area and Circumference of a Circle

This Console Application solution takes a single value and outputs the two calculated values. Note the use of a constant to hold the value of pi.

```vbnet
Module Module1
    'Declaration of Pi as a CONSTANT as the value will not change
    Const Pi As Decimal = 3.14159

    Sub Main()

        'Declaration of Local Variables
        Dim Radius As Decimal = 0
        Dim Area As Decimal = 0
        Dim Circumference As Decimal = 0

        'Obtain user input and pass to variable
        Console.WriteLine("Enter Radius")
        Radius = Console.ReadLine

        'Storing the calculated value for area in the local variable
        Area = Pi * Radius * Radius
```

```
                'Storing the calculated value for circumference in the local variable
                Circumference = 2 * Pi * Radius

                'Output the values held in local variables to the console
                Console.WriteLine(Area)
                Console.WriteLine(Circumference)

                Console.ReadKey()

        End Sub
End Module
```

A Windows Form application could use two buttons allowing the user to input a single value and select the required output.

Figure 13.02 shows an example of the interface that could be used with this task.

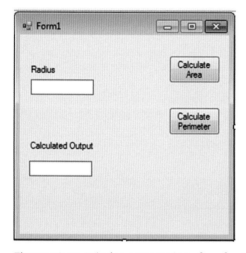

Figure 13.02 Windows Forms interface for Circle task

```
Public Class Form1
        'Declaration of Pi as a CONSTANT as the value will not change
        Const Pi As Decimal = 3.14159

        'Declaration of Radius as a GLOBAL VARIABLE so it can be accessed by both subroutines
        Dim Radius As Decimal = 0

        Private Sub BTNCalc _ Click(sender As Object, e As EventArgs) Handles BTNCalcArea.Click

                'Declaration of LOCAL VARIABLE
                Dim Area As Decimal = 0

                'Obtaining input data from user via the Textbox
                Radius = TBRadius.Text

                'Storing the calculated value for area in the local variable
                Area = Pi * Radius * Radius

                'Output the value held in local variable to the Textbox
                TBOutput.Text = Area

        End Sub

        Private Sub BTNCalcPerimeter _ Click(sender As Object, e As EventArgs) Handles
        BTNCalcPerimeter.Click
                'Declaration of LOCAL VARIABLE
                Dim Circumference As Decimal = 0
```

```
'Obtaining input data from user via the Textbox
Radius = TBRadius.Text

'Storing the calculated value for circumference in the local variable
Circumference = 2 * Pi * Radius

'Output the value held in local variable to the Textbox
TBOutput.Text = Circumference
    End Sub
End Class
```

Chapter 4 Selection

Discussion Questions

1   The output will remain the same if the criteria is reversed. The crucial values to consider are where Number1 and Number2 are identical. The IF statement criteria will only be true where Number2 is greater than Number1. Therefore where both numbers are identical the criteria will be false and the ELSE element of the IF statement will be followed resulting in an output of "FIRST"

If the criteria are reversed, identical numbers will still fail to meet the criteria and the algorithm will still follow the ELSE path.

2   **a**   The logical operator would need to change to IF Number2 >= Number1, identical number will meet the criteria resulting in an output of "SECOND"

b   If the criteria are reversed, IF Number1 <= Number2, identical numbers will still meet the criteria and the algorithm will output "SECOND"

Parcel Delivery System

Figure 13.03 shows a flowchart and a pseudocode design for this task.

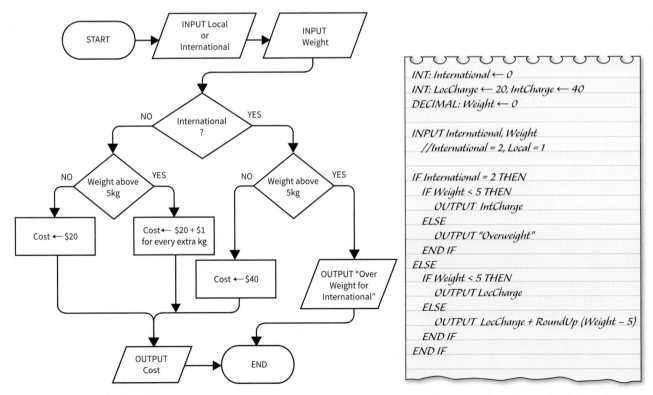

Figure 13.03 Flowchart and pseudocode for parcel delivery system

The following Visual Basic solution makes use of NESTED IF statements:

```
Module Module1
    Sub Main()
        Dim International As Integer = 0
        Dim Weight As Decimal = 0
        'Declaring the fixed charges as constants as values will not
         Change during execution of the code
        Const IntCharge As Integer = 40
        Const LocCharge As Integer = 20

        Console.WriteLine("Select Local or International")
        Console.WriteLine("1 = Local")
        Console.WriteLine("2 = International")
        International = Console.ReadLine

        Console.WriteLine("Insert Weight")
        Weight = Console.ReadLine

        If International = 2 Then 'Start of main IF statement
            If Weight <= 5 Then 'Start on first nested IF
                Console.WriteLine(IntCharge)
            Else
                Console.WriteLine("Over Weight")
            End If
        Else
            If Weight <= 5 Then 'Start of 2nd nested IF
                Console.WriteLine(LocCharge)
            Else
                Console.WriteLine(LocCharge + Math.Ceiling(Weight - 5))
                'Use of the Math class library which provides
                 mathematical methods. Method selected is 'ceiling' which
                 rounds up to nearest integer
            End If
        End If
        Console.ReadKey()
    End Sub
End Module
```

It would not have been possible to use a simple CASE statement in this problem because the selection criteria are based on more than one variable. However nested CASE statements are possible:

```
Select Case International
    Case Is = 2
        Select Case Weight
            Case Weight <= 5
                Console.WriteLine(IntCharge)
            Case Else
                Console.WriteLine("Over Weight")
        End Select
    Case Else
        Select Case Weight
            Case Weight <= 5
                Console.WriteLine(LocCharge)
            Case Else
                Console.WriteLine(LocCharge + Math.Ceiling(Weight - 5))
        End Select
End Select
```

CO$_2$ Calculator

Figure 13.04 shows a flowchart and a pseudocode design for this task.

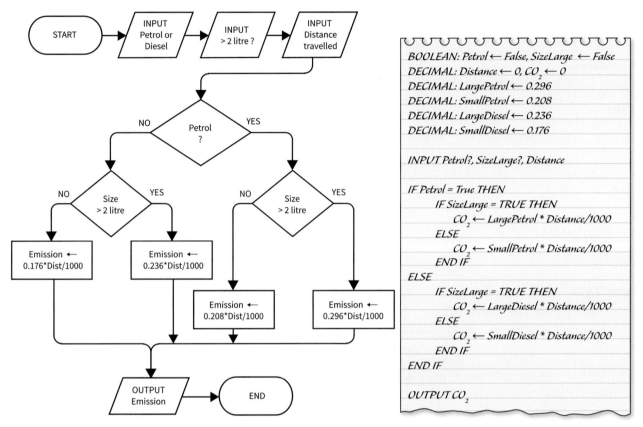

BOOLEAN: Petrol ← False, SizeLarge ← False
DECIMAL: Distance ← 0, CO$_2$ ← 0
DECIMAL: LargePetrol ← 0.296
DECIMAL: SmallPetrol ← 0.208
DECIMAL: LargeDiesel ← 0.236
DECIMAL: SmallDiesel ← 0.176

INPUT Petrol?, SizeLarge?, Distance

IF Petrol = True THEN
    IF SizeLarge = TRUE THEN
        CO$_2$ ← LargePetrol * Distance/1000
    ELSE
        CO$_2$ ← SmallPetrol * Distance/1000
    END IF
ELSE
    IF SizeLarge = TRUE THEN
        CO$_2$ ← LargeDiesel * Distance/1000
    ELSE
        CO$_2$ ← SmallDiesel * Distance/1000
    END IF
END IF

OUTPUT CO$_2$

Figure 13.04 Flow Chart and pseudo code for CO$_2$ Calculator algorithm

The following is a possible Visual Basic solution:

```
Module Module1
    Sub Main()
        Dim Petrol As Boolean = False
        Dim SizeLarge As Boolean = False
        Dim Distance As Decimal = 0
        Dim CO2 As Decimal = 0
        Const LargePetrol As Decimal = 0.296
        Const SmallPetrol As Decimal = 0.208
        Const LargeDiesel As Decimal = 0.236
        Const SmallDiesel As Decimal = 0.176

        Console.WriteLine("Is your vehicle Petrol?")
        Console.WriteLine("INPUT    YES    or    NO")

        If Console.ReadLine = "YES" Then
            Petrol = True
        Else
            Petrol = False
        End If

        Console.WriteLine("Is your vehicle larger than 2 litres?")
        Console.WriteLine("INPUT    YES    or    NO")

        If Console.ReadLine = "YES" Then
            SizeLarge = True
        Else
```

```
            SizeLarge = False
        End If

        Console.WriteLine("Input annual Mileage")
        Distance = Console.ReadLine()

        If Petrol = True Then
            If SizeLarge = True Then
                CO2 = LargePetrol * Distance / 1000
            Else
                CO2 = SmallPetrol * Distance / 1000
            End If
        Else
            If SizeLarge = True Then
                CO2 = LargeDiesel * Distance / 1000
            Else
                CO2 = SmallDiesel * Distance / 1000
            End If
        End If

        Console.WriteLine(CO2)
        Console.ReadKey()
    End Sub
End Module
```

Calculator Task

Figure 13.05 shows a flowchart for this task.

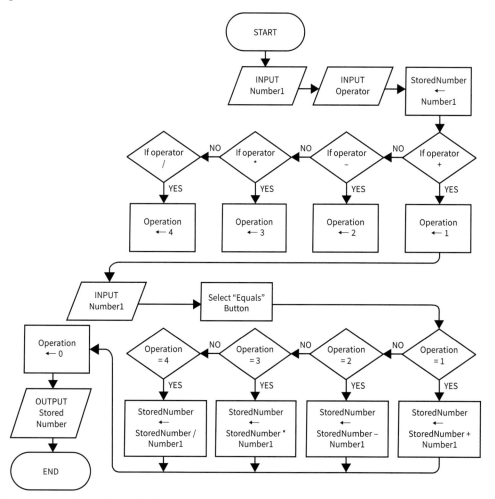

Figure 13.05 Flow Chart of Calculator algorithm

The following is a possible Visual Basic solution for the Add button, which is repeated for the Subtract, Multiply and Divide buttons:

```
Public Class Form1
    Dim Operation As Integer = 0
    Dim Number1 As Decimal = 0
    Dim Number2 As Decimal = 0
    Dim Answer As Decimal = 0

    Private Sub BTNAdd _ Click(sender As Object, e As EventArgs) Handles BTNAdd.Click
        'Stores the value from the textbox in the variable
        Number1 = TBInOut.Text
        'Sets the Variable to indicate selection
        Operation = 1
        'Clears the first number from the input/output box
        TBInOut.Text = ""
        Me.ActiveControl = TBInOut
    End Sub
```

Figure 13.06(a) shows a possible Visual Basic solution for the Equals button using an IF..ELSE IF..ELSE..ENDIF statement and Figure 13.06(b) implements it using a CASE statement.

```
Private Sub BTNEquals_Click(sender As Object,
        e As EventArgs) Handles BTNEquals.Click
    'Stores the second number in variable
    Number2 = TBInOut.Text

    If Operation = 1 Then
        Answer = Number1 + Number2
        TBInOut.Text = Answer
    ElseIf Operation = 2 Then
        Answer = Number1 - Number2
        TBInOut.Text = Answer
    ElseIf Operation = 3 Then
        Answer = Number1 * Number2
        TBInOut.Text = Answer
    ElseIf Operation = 4 Then
        Answer = Number1 / Number2
        TBInOut.Text = Answer
    Else
        MsgBox("Select Operator")
    End If
End Sub
```

(a)

```
Private Sub BTNEquals_Click(sender As Object,
            e As EventArgs) Handles
BTNEquals.Click
    'Stores the second number in variable
    Number2 = TBInOut.Text

    Select Case Operation
      Case Is = 1
        Answer = Number1 + Number2
        TBInOut.Text = Answer
      Case Is = 2
        Answer = Number1 - Number2
        TBInOut.Text = Answer
      Case Is = 3
        Answer = Number1 * Number2
        TBInOut.Text = Answer
      Case Is = 4
        Answer = Number1 / Number2
        TBInOut.Text = Answer
      Case Else
        MsgBox("Select Operator")
    End Select
End Sub
```

(b)

Figure 13.06 Code showing IF ELSE and CASE approach

The following is a possible Visual Basic solution for the Clear button:

```
    Private Sub BTNClear _ Click(sender As Object, e As EventArgs) Handles BTNClear.Click
        'Clears the answer from the input/output box
        TBInOut.Text = ""
        Me.ActiveControl = TBInOut
    End Sub
End Class
```

CO$_2$ Calculator Extension Task

```
If Petrol = True And SizeLarge = True Then
        CO₂ = LargePetrol * Distance / 1000
Else
        If Petrol = True And SizeLarge = False Then
                CO₂ = SmallPetrol * Distance / 1000
        Else
                If Petrol = False And SizeLarge = True Then
                        CO₂ = LargeDiesel * Distance / 1000
                Else
                        CO₂ = SmallDiesel * Distance / 1000
                End If
        End If
End If
```

Calculator Extension Task

Figure 13.07 shows a flowchart for this task. When diagrams become complex it is normal to separate them into different diagrams. The circle shape indicates where the individual diagrams connect.

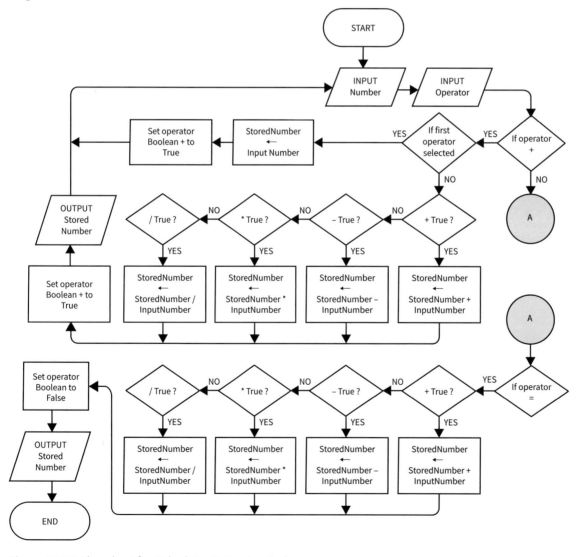

Figure 13.07 Flowchart for Calculator Extension Task

This is only part of the complete flowchart. The full chart would include the flow for all of the four operators. In this scenario an individual flow chart for each of the event buttons would be a good option. Use the circle symbol (a connector) to indicate where the individual diagrams join.

The following code shows a possible solution using Boolean values to identify which operator has been selected. A String or Integer variable could also have been used.

```
Public Class Form1

    Dim Add As Boolean = False
    Dim Subt As Boolean = False
    Dim Multi As Boolean = False
    Dim Div As Boolean = False
    Dim Number1 As Decimal = 0
    Dim Number2 As Decimal = 0
    Dim Answer As Decimal = 0

    Private Sub Form1 _ Load(sender As Object, e As EventArgs) Handles Me.Load
        'Set the Textbox as the active control
        'automatically placing the curser in the box ready for data entry
        Me.ActiveControl = TBInOut
    End Sub

    Private Sub BTNAdd _ Click(sender As Object, e As EventArgs) Handles BTNAdd.Click

        'If the first operator then all operator booleans will be False
        'Use conditions combined with AND to check all are False
        'If all False then store the value from the textbox in the variable
        If Add = False And Subt = False And Multi = False And Div = False Then
            Number1 = TBInOut.Text
            TBInOut.Text = ""
        Else
            'Stores the current number input into the variable
            Number2 = TBInOut.Text
            'Nested IF statement will run if one of the Booleans is True
            'IF-ELSEIF statement checks all Booleans completing the appropriate operation
            'and displays the result in the textbox
            If Add = True Then
                Answer = Number1 + Number2
                TBInOut.Text = Answer
            ElseIf Subt = True Then
                Answer = Number1 - Number2
                TBInOut.Text = Answer
            ElseIf Multi = True Then
                Answer = Number1 * Number2
                TBInOut.Text = Answer
            ElseIf Div = True Then
                Answer = Number1 / Number2
                TBInOut.Text = Answer
            End If
            'Copies the value of the latest operation to Number1 to maintain cumulative total
            Number1 = Answer
        End If

        'Sets the Booleans to indicate the latest selection and clears previous selection
        Add = True
        Subt = False
        Multi = False
        Div = False

        'gives the textbox focus
        Me.ActiveControl = TBInOut
    End Sub
```

The subroutine above for the Add button is repeated for the Subtract, Multiply and Divide buttons. The following code shows a possible solution for the Equals and Clear buttons.

```
Private Sub BTNEquals _ Click(sender As Object, e As EventArgs) Handles BTNEquals.Click
    Number2 = TBInOut.Text

    If Add = True Then
        Answer = Number1 + Number2
        TBInOut.Text = Answer
    ElseIf Subt = True Then
        Answer = Number1 - Number2
        TBInOut.Text = Answer
    ElseIf Multi = True Then
        Answer = Number1 * Number2
        TBInOut.Text = Answer
    ElseIf Div = True Then
        Answer = Number1 / Number2
        TBInOut.Text = Answer
    End If

    'Sets all the boolean values to False as sequence ended
    Add = False
    Subt = False
    Multi = False
    Div = False
End Sub

Private Sub BTNClear _ Click(sender As Object, e As EventArgs) Handles BTNClear.Click
    'Sets all Boolean values back to False
    Add = False
    Subt = False
    Multi = False
    Div = False
    'Clears the answer from the input/output box
    TBInOut.Text = ""
    Me.ActiveControl = TBInOut
End Sub
End Class
```

Chapter 5 Iteration

FOR Loop Tasks

1 Figures 13.08 and 13.09 show the output screens for Console and Windows Forms solutions.

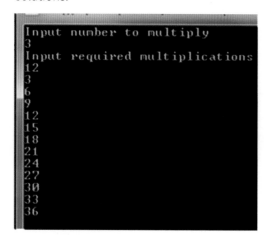

Figure 13.08 Console output

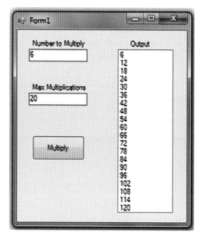

Figure 13.09 Windows Forms interface

Figure 13.10(a) shows the code for the Console Application and Figure 13.10(b) shows the code for the Windows Forms Application.

```
Module Module1
    Sub Main()
        Dim Multiply As Integer
        Dim MaxMulti As Integer

        Console.WriteLine("Input number to
            multiply")
        Multiply = Console.ReadLine
        Console.WriteLine("Input required
            multiplications")
        MaxMulti = Console.ReadLine

        For i = 1 To MaxMulti
            Console.WriteLine(Multiply * i)
        Next

        Console.ReadKey()
    End Sub
End Module
```

```
Public Class Form1
    Dim Multiply As Integer
    Dim MaxMulti As Integer

    Private Sub BTNMultiply_Click(sender As Object,
                        e As EventArgs) Handles
BTNMultiply.Click
        Multiply = TBInput.Text
        MaxMulti = TBMaxMulti.Text

        If a listbox is not cleared the list will
continue
        to extend with each new event
        ListBoxOutput.Items.Clear()

        For i = 1 To MaxMulti
            ListBoxOutput.Items.Add(Multiply * i)
        Next

    End Sub
End Class
```

(a)   **(b)**

Figure 13.10 Visual Basic code for Console and Windows Forms application

2   Figures 13.11 and 13.12 show the output screens for Console and Windows Forms solutions.

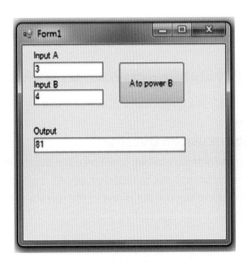

Figure 13.11 Console interface

Figure 13.12 Windows Forms interface

Figure 13.13(a) shows the code for the Console Application and Figure 13.13(b) shows the code for the Windows Forms Application.

```
Module Module1                              Public Class Form1
    Sub Main()
        Dim NumA As Integer = 0                 Dim NumA As Integer = 0
        Dim NumB As Integer = 0                 Dim NumB As Integer = 0

        Console.WriteLine                       Private Sub BTNPower_Click(sender As Object,
            ("Insert X - Number value in X to the power Y")          e As EventArgs) Handles
        NumA = Console.ReadLine                      BTNPower.Click
        Console.WriteLine                            NumA = TBNumA.Text
            ("Insert Y - Power value in X to the power Y")           NumB = TBNumB.Text
        NumB = Console.ReadLine
                                                    Dim NumAPower As Integer = 0
        'Declare local variable to use in the process
        Dim NumAPower As Integer = 0                For i = 2 To NumB
                                                        If i = 2 Then
        'FOR loop to iterate up to NumB times                NumAPower = NumA * NumA
        'Note the start value of 2 because NumA             Else
        'to power 1 = NumA                                      NumAPower = NumAPower * NumA
        For i = 2 To NumB                               End If
            'Use of an IF statement to identify if first    Next
            'iteration - new variable needs to be used to   TBOutput.Text = NumAPower
            'hold NumA squared. Subsequent iteration will   End Sub
            'multiply the new variable by NumA          End Class
            If i = 2 Then
                NumAPower = NumA * NumA
            Else
                NumAPower = NumAPower * NumA
            End If
        Next
        Console.WriteLine(NumAPower)
        Console.ReadKey()
    End Sub
End Module
```

(a)   **(b)**

Figure 13.13 Visual Basic code for Console and Windows Forms approach

In Visual Basic you can generate powers by use of the ^ symbol, 2^3 = 8.

Prime Task Discussion Question

Limiting the iterations to Number -1 will result in iterations where the counter value is greater than half of the input number. In those situations it would be impossible to produce a modulus of zero. Limiting the iterations to the rounded integer value of Number / 2 would be more efficient.

Prime Number Extension Task

The following code shows how the original code could be altered to implement the required output of positive divisors. It makes use of the visibility method of a listbox object. It is also a good example of effective sequence by ensuring that the two outputs are included in the correct code sequence. The output of positive divisors included within the loop but the final indication of Prime identified once the loop has completed.

```
Public Class Form1
    'Comments only show changes from code in Prime Task
    Dim NumberIn As Integer = 0

    Private Sub BTNPrime _ Click(sender As Object, e As EventArgs) Handles BTNPrime.Click

        Dim Modulus As Integer = 0
        Dim ModCount As Integer = 0

        'Listbox is cleared of any values from previous input numbers
        LBDivisors.Items.Clear()
```

```
        NumberIn = TBInput.Text

        'The range of the FOR loop is limited to hald of the input number
        'Any number greater than half of the input number cannot be a positive divisor
        For i = 2 To NumberIn / 2

            Modulus = NumberIn Mod i

        If Modulus = 0 Then
            ModCount = ModCount + 1
            Original code altered to add the counter value of i to the listbox
            '   when the modulus is 0 which indicates a psoitive divisor
            LBDivisors.Items.Add(i)
        End If

        Next

        If ModCount = 0 Then
            TBOutput.Text = "This is a PRIME number"
            'The visibility property is used to hide the listbox
            LBDivisors.Visible = False
        Else
            TBOutput.Text = "NOT a PRIME number"
            'The visibility property is used to display the listbox
            LBDivisors.Visible = True
        End If

    End Sub
End Class
```

WHILE Loop Task

Figure 13.14 shows the flowchart and pseudocode for the quotient and modulus calculator.

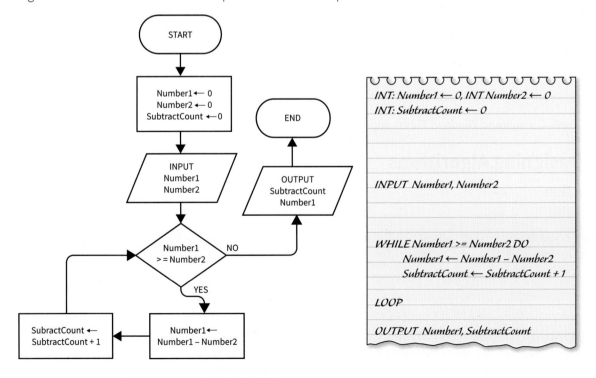

Figure 13.14 Flowchart and pseudocode for While loop

Figures 13.15 and 13.16 show the output screens for Console and Windows Forms solutions.

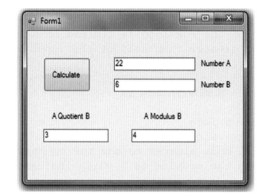

```
Input Number A
22
Input Number B
6
A Quotient B = 3
A Modulus B = 4
```

Figure 13.15 Console Window

Figure 13.16 Windows Forms interface

Figure 13.17(a) shows possible code for the Console Application and Figure 13.17(b) for the Windows Forms Application.

```
Module Module1
    Sub Main()
        Dim NumA As Integer = 0
        Dim NumB As Integer = 0
        Dim SubtractCounter As Integer = 0
        'Obtain and store input from user
        Console.WriteLine("Input Number A")
        NumA = Console.ReadLine
        Console.WriteLine("Input Number B")
        NumB = Console.ReadLine
        Do While NumA >= NumB
            'Within loop subtract NumB from NumA and
            'record number of iterations
            NumA = NumA - NumB
            SubtractCounter = SubtractCounter + 1
        Loop
        'Note the use of concatenation to join strings
        'and/or variables to create a longer string.
        'In VB.Net the & is the concatenation symbol
        Console.WriteLine("A Quotient B = "
            & SubtractCounter)
        Console.WriteLine("A Modulus B = " & NumA)
        Console.ReadKey()
    End Sub
End Module
```

```
Public Class Form1

    Private Sub BTNCalculate_Click(sender As Object,
                      e As EventArgs) Handles
BTNCalculate.Click
        Dim NumA As Integer = 0
        Dim NumB As Integer = 0
        Dim SubCounter As Integer = 0

        NumA = TBNumA.Text
        NumB = TBNumB.Text

        Do While NumA >= NumB
            NumA = NumA - NumB
            SubCounter = SubCounter + 1
        Loop

        TBQuotient.Text = SubCounter
        TBModulus.Text = NumA
    End Sub
End Class
```

(a)

(b)

Figure 13.17 Visual Basic Console and Windows Forms approach

Chapter 6 Designing Algorithms

Discussion Question

Other solutions include:

- The IF statement could determine the highest number input before the calculation of Total. Both must remain within the loop but the order of completion is not important.

- The FOR loop could have been written as FOR Counter = 0 To 99; this would still iterate 100 times.

- It would have been possible to use a WHILE or REPEAT..UNTIL loop. Although a FOR loop is an efficient solution to a scenario where the number of iterations is known any loop can be written to perform a similar role. Remember that in a FOR loop the NEXT statement automatically increments the loop counter; WHILE and REPEAT..UNTIL loops do not automatically increment the loop counter so this would need to be included in the code.

Design Challenge 1

Figure 13.18 shows a flowchart and pseudocode for the algorithm.

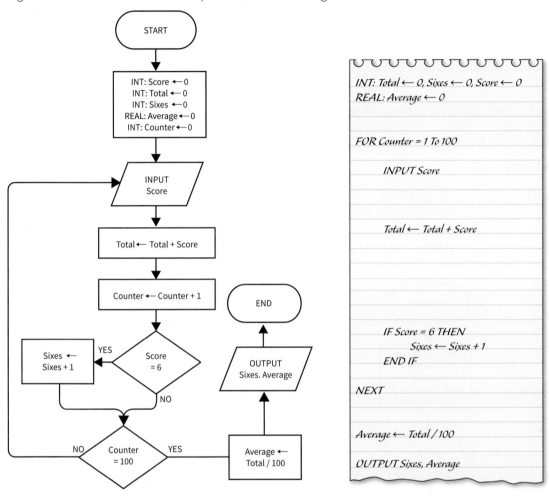

Figure 13.18 Flowchart and pseudocode example for Task 1

The algorithm uses a FOR loop as the number of iterations known. An IF statement is used to increment the record of sixes thrown. The average is calculated and displayed outside the loop.

The following code is an example of a solution using the console window. To test your code reduce the iterations to a much smaller number (for example, change the FOR loop to read For i = 1 To 5).

```
Module Module1
    Sub Main()
    'Declare and initialise required variables
    Dim Total As Integer = 0
    Dim Sixes As Integer = 0
    Dim Score As Integer = 0
    Dim Average As Decimal = 0

        'Start FOR Loop that will iterate 100 times
        For i = 1 To 100
            'Input score via the console
            Score = Console.ReadLine

            'Increment Total to maintain the sum of all inputs
            Total = Total + Score
```

```
        'If statement increments the record of sixes
        'when the score is equal to six
        If Score = 6 Then
            Sixes = Sixes + 1
        End If
    Next

    'Calculate average of all 100 inputs
    Average = Total / 100

    'Output the Average and the number of sixes
    Console.WriteLine(Average)
    Console.WriteLine(Sixes)

    Console.ReadKey()
    End Sub
End Module
```

Design Challenge 2

Figure 13.19 shows a flowchart for the algorithm: the loop is controlled by the condition Doubles = 100.

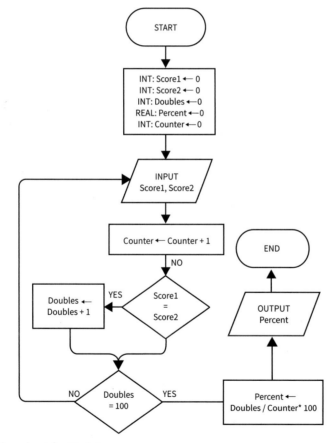

Figure 13.19 Flowchart for Task 2

Within the loop:

- The input of the score from both dice continues.
- A counter is incremented to maintain a record of how many throws have been recorded. This will be needed to calculate the final percentage value.
- A decision statement is used to increment the number of double scores (when both dice show the same number).

Once the loop condition has been met the percentage is calculated and output.

The two pseudocode solutions show how either a WHILE loop (Figure 13.20(a)) or a REPEAT.. UNTIL loop (Figure 13.20(b)) could be used to achieve the aim of the algorithm.

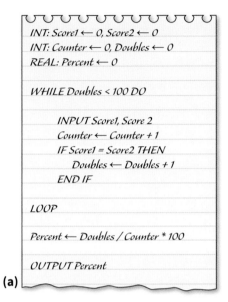

```
INT: Score1 ← 0, Score2 ← 0
INT: Counter ← 0, Doubles ← 0
REAL: Percent ← 0

WHILE Doubles < 100 DO

        INPUT Score1, Score 2
        Counter ← Counter + 1
        IF Score1 = Score2 THEN
            Doubles ← Doubles + 1
        END IF

LOOP

Percent ← Doubles / Counter * 100

OUTPUT Percent
```
(a)

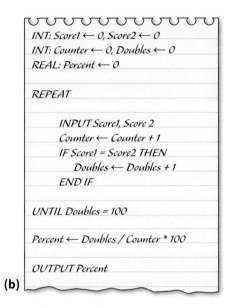

```
INT: Score1 ← 0, Score2 ← 0
INT: Counter ← 0, Doubles ← 0
REAL: Percent ← 0

REPEAT

        INPUT Score1, Score 2
        Counter ← Counter + 1
        IF Score1 = Score2 THEN
            Doubles ← Doubles + 1
        END IF

UNTIL Doubles = 100

Percent ← Doubles / Counter * 100

OUTPUT Percent
```
(b)

Figure 13.20 Pseudocode for WHILE and REPEAT..UNTIL approach

The following code is an example of a solution using the console window and a WHILE loop. To test your code reduce the iterations to a much smaller number, such as 5.

```
Module Module1
    Sub Main()
    'Declare and initialise required variables
    Dim Score1 As Integer = 0
    Dim Score2 As Integer = 0
    Dim Doubles As Integer = 0
    Dim Counter As Integer = 0
    Dim Percent As Decimal = 0

        'Start While loop
        Do While Doubles < 100

            'Input the scores on both dice via the console
            Score1 = Console.ReadLine
            Score2 = Console.ReadLine

            'Increment counter to record how many throws input
            Counter = Counter + 1

            'IF statement compares scores on the dice
            'and increments Doubles if the scores are the same
            If Score1 = Score2 Then
                Doubles = Doubles + 1
            End If
        Loop

        'Calculate percentage
        Percent = Doubles / Counter * 100
        Console.WriteLine(Percent)
        Console.ReadLine()
    End Sub
End Module
```

An UNTIL loop would follow a very similar approach with the logic for the condition being changed to allow the loop to continue until Doubles reaches 100.

```
Do
        Score1 = Console.ReadLine
        Score2 = Console.ReadLine

        Counter = Counter + 1

        If Score1 = Score2 Then
            Doubles = Doubles + 1
        End If

Loop Until Doubles = 100
```

Design Challenge 3

Figure 13.21 shows a flowchart for the algorithm: the loop is controlled by the condition Number = –1.

Prior to the loop the first number input is placed in both the Highest and Lowest variables. This will ensure that the final values of the variables will always fall within the range of numbers input. This is particularly important for Lowest as the initial value of 0 is very likely to be below the range of the numbers input. As a result it is possible that the decision 'Number < Lowest' will never be True and that Lowest will remain as 0. Another way to avoid this issue would be to initialise Lowest with a very high value, such as 1,000,000, which would be sufficient to ensure that it would be above the likely range of the numbers to be input.

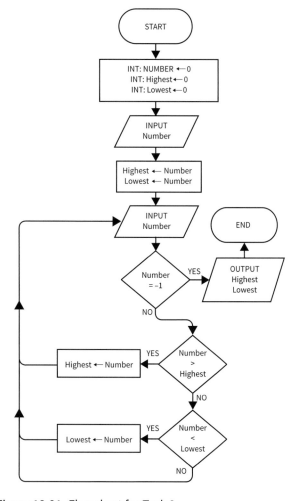

Figure 13.21 Flowchart for Task 3

The two pseudocode solutions show how either a WHILE loop (Figure 13.22(a)) or a REPEAT..
UNTIL loop (Figure 13.22(b)) could be used to achieve the aim of the algorithm.

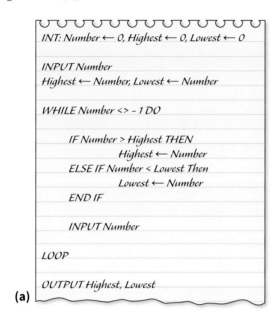

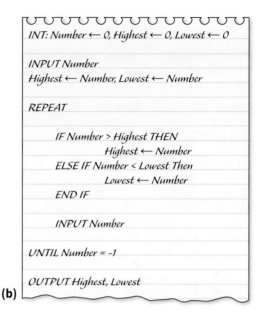

(a)　　　　　　　　　　　　　　　　　(b)

Figure 13.22 Pseudocode for WHILE and REPEAT..UNTIL approach to Task 3

A coded solution using a WHILE loop could be as follows:

```
Module Module1
    Sub Main()
    'Declare and initialise the variables
    Dim Number As Integer = 0
    Dim Highest As Integer = 0
    Dim Lowest As Integer = 0

        'Input first number
        Number = Console.ReadLine()

        'Use the first number to give variables a
        'value within the input range
        Highest = Number
        Lowest = Number
        'Start WHILE loop to continue while number is not - 1
        Do While Number <> -1

            'If statement to determine if new input is at
            'extreme of input range. If true value placed
            'in appropriate variable
            If Number > Highest Then
                Highest = Number
            ElseIf Number < Lowest Then
                Lowest = Number
            End If

            'Subsequent numbers input as part of loop
            Number = Console.ReadLine()
        Loop

        'Once loop ended by input of -1, values are output
        Console.WriteLine(Highest)
        Console.WriteLine(Lowest)

        Console.ReadKey()
    End Sub
End Module
```

A REPEAT..UNTIL loop would follow a very similar approach with the logic for the loop condition being changed to allow the loop to continue until the –1 input value is received.

```
Do
    If Number > Highest Then
        Highest = Number
    ElseIf Number < Lowest Then
        Lowest = Number
    End If

    Number = Console.ReadLine()

Loop Until Number = -1
```

Design Challenge 4

Figure 13.23 shows a flowchart and pseudocode for the algorithm: the loop is controlled by the input of 200 values.

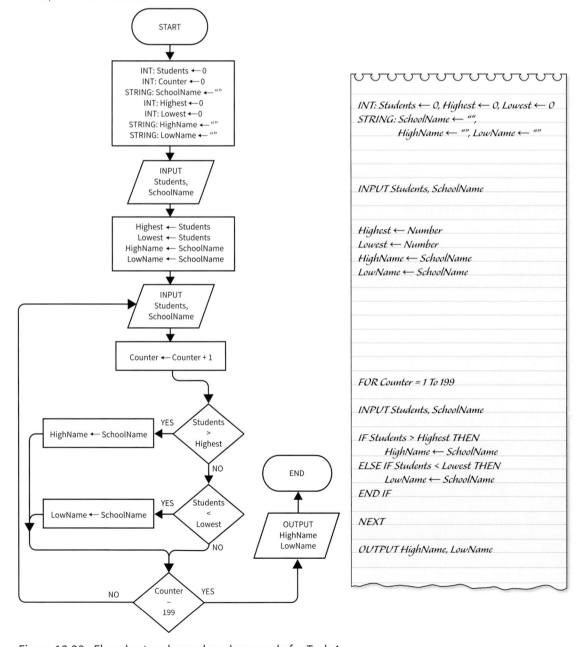

Figure 13.23   Flowchart and pseudocode example for Task 4

The algorithm passes the first input values to the variables to ensure their final values lie within the range of the input values.

The exit decision is based on the counter reaching 199 although the task indicates that 200 values are to be entered. This is to allow for the first values, which are input outside the loop. An alternative method would have been to initialise the counter with the value of 1 to account for the first input values.

The following code is an example of a solution using the console window. To test your code reduce the iterations to a much smaller number (for example, For i = 1 To 5).

```
Module Module1
    Sub Main()
    'Declare and initialise variables
    'note the use of the "" to indicate an empty string
    Dim Students As Integer = 0
    Dim Highest As Integer = 0
    Dim Lowest As Integer = 0
    Dim SchoolName As String = ""
    Dim HighName As String = ""
    Dim LowName As String = ""

        'Obtain the first input values - WriteLine used to give user instructions
        Console.WriteLine("Please type the number of students and select ENTER")
        Students = Console.ReadLine
        Console.WriteLine("Please type the name of the school and select ENTER")
        SchoolName = Console.ReadLine

        'Set variable values to first input values to ensure
        'variables are initialised with actual input values
        Highest = Students
        Lowest = Students
        HighName = SchoolName
        LowName = SchoolName

        'FOR loop to iterate 199 times - this is 1 less than the
        'required 200 because 1st input is outside the loop
        For i = 1 To 199

            'Obtain subsequent input values
            Console.WriteLine("Please type the number of students and select ENTER")
            Students = Console.ReadLine
            Console.WriteLine("Please type the name of the school and select ENTER")
            SchoolName = Console.ReadLine

            'IF - ELSEIF used to identify if number of students is the
            'highest or lowest. This could have been two independent IF
            'statements, but as the input cannot be both the largest and
            'smallest this is more efficient.
            If Students > Highest Then
                HighName = SchoolName
            ElseIf Students < Lowest Then
                LowName = SchoolName
            End If

        Next

        'Display the required outputs
        Console.WriteLine(HighName)
        Console.WriteLine(LowName)

        Console.ReadKey()
    End Sub
End Module
```

143

Design Challenge 5

Figure 13.24 shows a flowchart and pseudocode for the algorithm. The pseudocode uses a REPEAT..UNTIL loop.

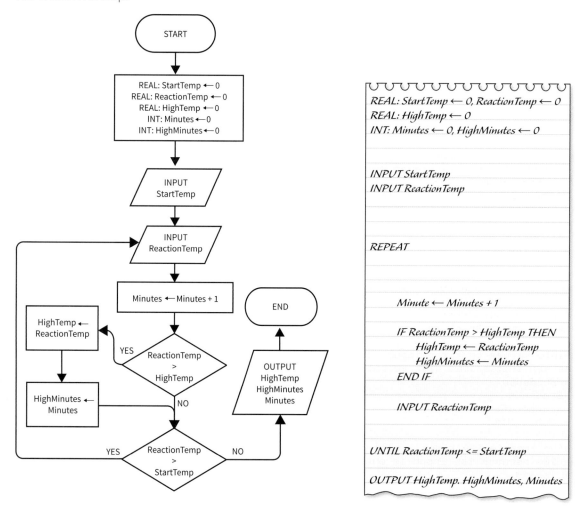

Figure 13.24 Flowchart and pseudocode examples for Task 5

The following code is an example of a solution using the console window.

```
Module Module1
    Sub Main()
    'Declare and initialise required variables
    'Temperatures declared as Decimal to allow fractions of a temperature unit
    Dim StartTemp As Decimal = 0
    Dim ReactionTemp As Decimal = 0
    Dim HighTemp As Decimal = 0
    Dim Minutes As Integer = 0
    Dim HighMinutes As Integer = 0

        'Input the start temperature outside loop
        Console.WriteLine("Please input the start temperature and select ENTER")
        StartTemp = Console.ReadLine

        Do
            'Reaction temperature(s) are input
            'In the scenario this would be automatic input from a sensor
            ReactionTemp = Console.ReadLine
```

```
        'Increment minutes by 1 every time a new reaction temperature is input
        Minutes = Minutes + 1

        'IF statement used to check if the reaction temperature is at its
        'highest value; if the condition is TRUE then the current values are
        'passed to HighTemp and HighMinutes variables
        If ReactionTemp > HighTemp Then
            HighTemp = ReactionTemp
            HighMinutes = Minutes
        End If

        'End of UNTIL loop will iterate execution of code to the start
        'of the loop, while the loop condition remains FALSE
    Loop Until ReactionTemp < StartTemp

    'Display the required outputs
    Console.WriteLine(HighTemp)
    Console.WriteLine(HighMinutes)
    Console.WriteLine(Minutes)

    Console.ReadKey()
    End Sub
End Module
```

A WHILE loop would follow a very similar approach with the logic for the loop condition being changed to allow the loop to continue WHILE the reaction temperature is greater than the starting temperature. The process is complicated because we need to input the first reaction temperature outside the loop to provide a value for the WHILE loop to evaluate. As the first value is obtained outside the loop the minutes counter must also be incremented outside the loop.

```
    ReactionTemp = Console.ReadLine
    Minutes = Minutes + 1

    Do While ReactionTemp > StartTemp

        If ReactionTemp > HighTemp Then
            HighTemp = ReactionTemp
            HighTime = Minutes
        End If

        ReactionTemp = Console.ReadLine
        Minutes = Minutes + 1
    Loop
```

Chapter 7 Subroutines

Produce Multiples Extension Task

The following pseudocode models the algorithm:

```
SUB Multiply (INT: Num1, INT: Num2)
    FOR i = 1 To Num2
        OUTPUT Num1 * i
    NEXT
END SUB
```

The following code is an example of a solution using the console window:

```
Module Module1
    Sub Main()

        Dim NumberToMultiply, Amount As Integer
        Console.WriteLine("Input the number to multiply")
        NumberToMultiply = Console.ReadLine
        Console.WriteLine("Input the amount of multiples to show")
        Amount = Console.ReadLine

        Call Multiply(NumberToMultiply, Amount)

        Console.ReadKey()

    End Sub
    Sub Multiply(Num1 As Integer, Num2 As Integer)
        For i = 1 To Num2
            Console.WriteLine(Num1 * i)
        Next

    End Sub
End Module
```

As you type in the call instruction the IDE will identify the parameters expected (Figure 13.25). The name of the variable containing the parameter value does not need to match the name used in the procedure. The use of the value is indicated by their location in the call. The first variable will pass the value to Num1 and the second to Num2.

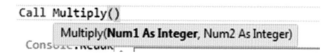

Figure 13.25 Identification of required parameters by IDE

Circumference and Area Extension Task

The following pseudocode shows the algorithm and the process of calling it:

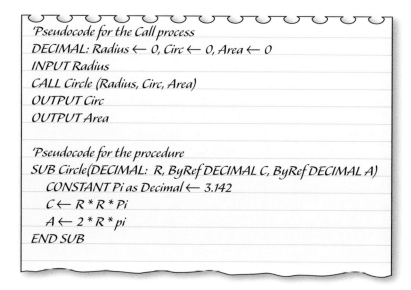

The following code is an example of a solution using the console window:

```
Module Module1
    Sub Main()
        Dim Radius, Circ, Area As Decimal
        Console.WriteLine("Insert value of radius")
        Radius = Console.ReadLine
        'Call the procedure providing required parameters
        Call Circle(Radius, Circ, Area)

        Console.WriteLine(Circ)
        Console.WriteLine(Area)
        Console.ReadKey()
    End Sub

    'Define the procedure
    'Note the use of ByRef to indicate the required return parameters
    'The procedure will:
    '- receive the parameter value R
    '- complete the processing to calculate C and A
    '- return those values by updating the values in the references (Circ and Area).
    Sub Circle(R As Decimal, ByRef C As Decimal, ByRef A As Decimal)
        Const Pi As Decimal = 3.142
        C = R * R * Pi
        A = 2 * Pi * R
    End Sub
End Module
```

Chapter 8 Checking Inputs

Validation Task 1

Figure 13.26 shows a flowchart and pseudocode for the algorithm.

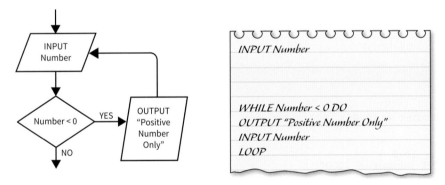

Figure 13.26 Flowchart and pseudocode for Task 1

The following code is an example of a solution using the console window.

```
Module Module1
    Sub Main()
        Dim Number As Decimal

        Console.WriteLine("Insert POSITIVE Number")
        Number = Console.ReadLine

        While Number < 0
            Console.WriteLine("POSITIVE Number only")
            Number = Console.ReadLine
        End While

    End Sub
End Module
```

147

This validation routine (and the one for Validation Task 2) will check the size of a numeric input but it will crash if a textual value is input. This is because the input value has to be passed to the variable before the validation check can be completed. As the Decimal data type cannot accept textual data the system will cause a data type error.

To solve this problem the input should first be validated to check that it is numeric. This could be achieved by the following process (see Validation Task 2 for a code implementation):

1 Accept the user input as a String variable.

2 Validate until the input is numeric.

3 Pass the numeric value to a variable of a numeric data type.

4 Check if the data meets any size conditions.

Validation Task 2

Figure 13.27 shows a flowchart and pseudocode for the algorithm.

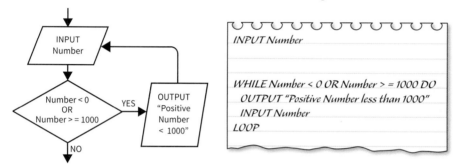

Figure 13.27 Flowchart and pseudocode for Task 2

The following code is an example of a solution using the console window.

```
Module Module1
    Sub Main()
        Dim Number As Decimal

        Console.WriteLine("POSITIVE Number < 1000")
        Number = Console.ReadLine

        While Number < 0 Or Number >= 1000
            Console.WriteLine("POSITIVE Number < 1000")
            Number = Console.ReadLine
        End While

    End Sub
End Module
```

This validation routine has the same problem as the one for Validation Task 1 if a textual value is input. The following code implements the additional validation process:

```
Sub Main()
        Dim Number As Integer
        Dim TempNumber As String

        Console.WriteLine("POSITIVE Number < 1000")
        TempNumber = Console.ReadLine

        While IsNumeric(TempNumber) = False
            Console.WriteLine("Numeric Value please")
            TempNumber = Console.ReadLine
        End While
        Number = TempNumber

        'continued validation

    End Sub
```

While this solution would work it is not entirely robust. Consider the situation where the user inputs a value that passes the numeric validation but then fails the size validation. The user will be prompted to input again; should the user input textual data the system will fail as the numeric check sequence has already been passed.

An effective solution to this problem is to make use of a function to complete the validation. The validation routine can be called until the data input meets the validation rules. It would not be possible to simply place this code directly into the main routine. As it is an IF statement it could only be executed once in the code sequence. Using a function allows repetitive calling.

```
Function Validate(ByVal I As String) As Boolean
    Dim N As Decimal
    If IsNumeric(I) = False Then
        Return False
    Else
        N = I
        If N < 0 Or N >= 1000 Then
            Return False
        Else
            Return True
        End If
    End If
End Function
Module Module1
    Sub Main()
        Dim Number As Integer
        Dim TempNumber As String

        Console.WriteLine("POSITIVE Number < 1000")
        TempNumber = Console.ReadLine
        'Function Validate is passed parameter of the
        'user input. Control is passed to the function which
        'will Return True/False.
        'If False is returned, input is requested
        While Validate(TempNumber) = False
            Console.WriteLine("POSITIVE Number < 1000")
            TempNumber = Console.ReadLine
        End While
        'Once data is validated by the function
        'data is passed to a variable of numeric data type
        Number = TempNumber

    End Sub
```

Validation Task 3 The flowchart and pseudocode solutions are the same as in Validation Task 2.

```
Private Sub Button1_Click(sender As Object, e As EventArgs) Handles Button1.Click
    Dim Num As Decimal
    Num = TBNumber.Text
    'Size validation completed
    If Num < 0 OR > 1000 Then
        'IF FAIL error message output and Routine halted
        'until user triggers event again
        MsgBox("POSITIVE value < 1000")
        Exit Sub
    End If
End Sub
```

Because the program will run and display the GUI it is possible to halt specific event-driven subroutines without stopping the entire program. This will allow user to re-input data and trigger the event again. The **Exit Sub** command used in these solutions will end the event-driven routine once the validation condition fails. This will prevent the remaining code from being executed with invalid data.

If textual data is input the system will give a data type exception error and crash. To avoid this additional validation is created to check the data type.

```
Private Sub Button1 _ Click(sender As Object, e As EventArgs) Handles Button1.Click
    Dim Num As Decimal

    'IF statement check for numeric input
    If IsNumeric(TBNumber.Text) = False Then
        'IF FAIL error message output and Routine halted
        'until user triggers event again
        MsgBox("Numeric Values ONLY")
        Exit Sub
    Else
        'If numeric validation check passed
        'value from textbox passed to variable
        Num = TBNumber.Text
        'Size validation completed
        If Num < 0 OR > 1000 Then
            'IF FAIL error message output and Routine halted
            'until user triggers event again
            MsgBox("POSITIVE value < 1000")
            Exit Sub
        End If
    End If
End Sub
```

In this solution nested IF statements are used to complete both validations. The IF statements check if the input value fails and halt the subroutine. The first IF statement checks the data type of the data in the text box. Once this is complete the data is passed to a variable to check the size validation rule.

Validation Task 4

Figure 13.28 shows a flowchart and pseudocode for the algorithm.

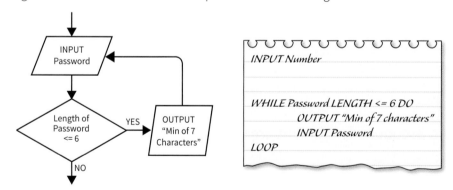

Figure 13.28 Flowchart and pseudocode for Task 4

The following code is an example of a solution using the console window:

```
Sub Main()
    Dim PW As String

    Console.WriteLine("Insert Password")
    PW = Console.ReadLine

a                                                    b
    While PW.Length <= 6
        Console.WriteLine("Must be at least 7 characters")
        Console.WriteLine("Insert Password")
        PW = Console.ReadLine
    End While
End Sub
```

The following code is an example of a Windows Forms Application solution:

```
Private Sub Button1_Click(sender As Object, e As EventArgs) Handles Button1.Click
    Dim PW As String
    PW = TBPassword.Text

    If PW.Length <= 6 Then
        MsgBox("Must be at least 7 characters")
        Exit Sub
    End If
End Sub
```

Validation Task 5

The following code is one possible solution for the function:

```
Function Validate(ByVal Number As Integer, ByVal PW As String) As Boolean
    If PW.Length <= 5 Then
        Return False
    Else
        If Number < 1000 Or Number > 1500 Then
            Return False
        Else
            Return True
        End If
    End If
End Function
```

If the subroutine also needed to return a specific error message, it would have to be a procedure as it would be required to return two values. Functions can only return one parameter value.

Validation Task 6

Figure 13.29(a) shows the flowchart for the main program. Note the symbol used to indicate a call to a subroutine. Figure 13.29(b) shows the flowchart for the function.

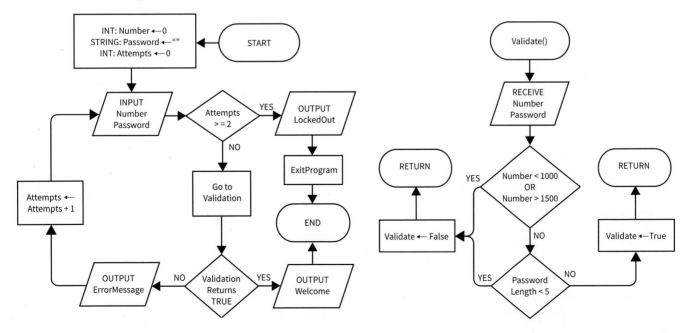

Figure 13.29 Flowcharts of the main program and function for Task 6

The following pseudocode is for the main program:

```
INT: Number ← 0, Attempts ← 0
STRING: Password ← ""

INPUT Number, Password

WHILE Validate (Number, Password) = False AND Attempts < 2  DO
    Attempts ← Attempts + 1
    If Attempts = 2 THEN
        OUTPUT "Locked Out"
        END Program
    ELSE
        OUTPUT "Incorrect Entry Please Re-enter"
        OUPUT "Password more than 5 characters"
        OUTPUT "Number between 1000 and 1500"
        INPUT Number Password
    END IF
LOOP

OUPUT "Welcome"
```

The following code is an example of a solution using the console window:

```
Sub Main()
    Dim PW As String = ""
    Dim Number As Integer = 0
    Dim Attempts As Integer = 0

    Console.WriteLine("Insert Password")
    PW = Console.ReadLine
    Console.WriteLine("Insert Number")
    Number = Console.ReadLine

    While Validate(Number, PW) = False And Attempts < 2
        Attempts = Attempts + 1
        If Attempts = 2 Then
            Console.WriteLine("Locked Out")
            Exit Sub
        Else
            Console.WriteLine("Incorrect please re-enter")
            Console.WriteLine("Password more than 5 characters")
            PW = Console.ReadLine
            Console.WriteLine("Number between 1000 and 1500")
            Number = Console.ReadLine
        End If
    End While

    Console.WriteLine("Welcome")
    Console.ReadKey()
End Sub
```

The program prompts user for input and uses a WHILE loop to iterate validation. Within the WHILE loop the main routine checks how many failed attempts have taken place. It uses the `Exit Sub` command to end the program.

The Validate function from Task 5 is used to complete all the size-related validation.

Chapter 9 Testing

Trace Table Extension Task

X	Y	W	Output	Comments
0	0	0		Initialisation values of the variables.
60	15	0		The new values are input.
45	15	1		X is reduced by 15, W is incremented by 1.
				Loop returns to the WHILE condition check. As X > Y, loop runs.
30	15	2		X is reduced by 15, W is incremented by 1.
				Loop returns to the WHILE condition check. As X > Y, loop runs.
15	15	3		X is reduced by 15, W is incremented by 1.
				Loop returns to the WHILE condition check. As X = Y, loop exits.
			3	The value in W is output.

The output is incorrect as 60 quotient 15 = 4. The error is in the last iteration – the loop condition should read WHILE X >= Y.

Discussion Question

The program returns the value A^5. Use of a trace table with different input values would help to determine the intention of the program.

Breakpoint Task

1 Tins of paint have been correctly declared as an integer, as you cannot get a fraction of a tin of paint. The system makes use of a simple division to calculate the number of tins of paint required which means that the resultant value will be rounded to an integer. In some test cases this will result in the number of tins being rounded down.

Using inputs of length 4.9 metres, height 2 metres and cover of 4 square metres, will produce an answer of two tins. The expected output is three tins (4.9 * 2 / 4 = 2.45, which must be rounded up to 3). For test data where the fraction of a tin calculated is 0.5 or more the problem does not exist.

2 To resolve the bug, the number of tins calculated always needs to be rounded up. This could be achieved in pseudocode by the use of an indication of ROUND UP. In Visual Basic the problem could be solved by using the maths library Ceiling method, which rounds to an integer value.

```
Tins = Math.Ceiling(Area / Cover)
```

Beta Testing Task

Mobile Telephone Number is a pseudo-number, not used for calculations and containing leading zeroes so the most appropriate type is String.

Validation	Invalid data	Boundary data
Length Entry must be 12 characters long	07736 123456789 (over length) 07736 123 (under length)	Entries of 11, 12 and 13 characters
Format check The system stipulates the format: NNNNN–NNNNNN	077–36123456 07736 123456 077361–23456 +44 7736–123456	Not relevant
Type check Must only contain digits	07736–ABCDEF	Not relevant
Presence check	Null input – leave the input blank	Not relevant

Note: A range check would not be appropriate as the data is not of a true numeric format.

Age Next Birthday must be a whole number so the most appropriate type is Integer.

Validation	Invalid data	Boundary data
Type check Data must be an integer	16.75 (must be whole number) Ten (must be a numeric value)	Not relevant
Range check The range should have reasonable minimum and maximum levels. The youngest patient could be newly born with an Age Next Birthday of 1. The other extreme could be set based on the maximum life expectancy; 110 would be reasonable.	–34 and 200 (Values well outside the expected boundaries)	0 and 1 (lower boundary) 109, 110 and 111 (upper boundary)
Presence check	Null input – leave the input blank	Not relevant

Testing Task 1

1 Input X = 16 and Y = 7

X	Y	W	Output	Comments
0	0	0		Initialisation values
16	7	7		X and Y are inputs, W = Y
9	7	14		X = X – Y, W = W + Y, Y unchanged Loops as X > 0
2	7	21		X = X – Y, W = W + Y, Y unchanged Loops as X > 0
–5	7	28		X = X – Y, W = W + Y, Y unchanged Loop ends as X < 0
			28	Value in W output

2 Input X = 10 and Y = 5

X	Y	W	Output	Comments
0	0	0		Initialisation values
10	5	5		X and Y Inputs , W = Y
5	5	10		X = X – Y, W = W + Y, Y unchanged Loops as X > 0
0	5	15		X = X – Y, W = W + Y, Y unchanged Loops as X = 0 (criteria in decision is X < 0)
–5	5	20		X = X – Y, W = W + Y, Y unchanged Loop ends as X < 0
			20	Value in W output

This is a typical exam-style question that has been set to test your understanding of the difference between < and <= in the decision criteria.

Testing Task 2

Error	Problem	Solution
`INT: Factorial ← 1`	The local declaration of the variable will result in its value being reset to 1 at every iteration of the loop.	Declaré Factorial as a global variable in the same way that Number has been declared.
`FOR Counter = 0 to Number`	Starting the iteration from zero will mean that Factorial will be set to zero at the first iteration. From that point onwards as Factorial is a multiple of itself the resultant multiplication will always be zero.	Set the iteration to run from 1: `FOR Counter = 1 to Number`
`Counter ← Counter + 1`	In a FOR loop, NEXT automatically increments the counter variable. As a result the loop will iterate with the value of Counter being incremented by 2 on each iteration.	Remove this line of code.

Testing Task 3

Error	Problem	Solution

`Small ← 0`	Initialising the variable to zero will mean that Small is always less than the value of any number input. As a result it will not record the lowest number.	1 Initialise Small with a large value
		`Small ← 100000`
		
		2 Set Small to the first Number input:
		`INPUT Number`
		`Small ← Number`
		`WHILE Number > 0`

`While Number > 0`	The input sequence should end when a negative number is input. The condition will end the loop when the user inputs a zero. Zero is not a negative number.	1 `While Number >= 0` 2 `While Number NOT < 0`
`Input Number`	There is no input of Number within the loop. As a result the value of Number will only ever be the first value input and the algorithm will be an infinite loop.	Accept the input of Number within the loop. It would be effective to add the line just before the LOOP terminator.

`Number ← Small`	Although the IF statement correctly checks the value of Number against the value of Small the action taken if Number is less than Small is incorrect. The assignment is the wrong way round – if the value of Small is assigned to Number, the lowest number would not be recorded and the incorrect value for Number would be used in the remaining code.	Change the assignment statement:
		
		`IF Number < Small THEN`
		`    Small ← Number`
		`END IF`

`OUTPUT Sum`	The output instruction is contained within the loop so the value of Sum will be output every iteration. Although the final value output will accurately represented the sum of all the numbers input, the algorithm was intended to output the final sum value only when the input sequence had ended.	Move this line out of the loop.

After making all those changes the corrected algorithm would look as follows:

```
INT: Number ← 0, Small ← 0, Sum ← 0
INPUT Number
Small ← Number
WHILE Number >= 0
    IF Number < Small THEN
        Small ← Number
    END IF
    Sum ← Sum + Number
    INPUT Number
LOOP
OUTPUT Sum
OUTPUT Small
```

Testing Task 4

Height in metres is likely to be a fractional value so the most appropriate type is Decimal, Real or Float.

Validation	Invalid data	Boundary data
Type check Data must be numeric	Two (must be a numeric value)	Not relevant
Range check The range should have reasonable minimum and maximum levels. The smallest height could be fairly low but not zero – A value of 0.5 could be reasonable. The other extreme could be set based on the maximum height of an adult – 2.6 metres would be reasonable. Other reasonable values are acceptable.	0.05 and 6 (values well outside the expected boundaries)	0.49, 0.5 and 0.51 (lower boundary) 2.59, 2.60 and 2.61 (upper boundary)
Presence check	Null input – leave the input blank	Not relevant

ID is a five-digit number. This might suggest an Integer but the scenario description does not exclude leading zeroes (00123 could be a valid ID) so the most appropriate type is String.

Validation	Invalid data	Boundary data
Type check Data must be numeric	1234A (must be a numeric value)	Not relevant
Length check Data must be five characters long	1234567 1234	Data of four, five and six characters
Presence check	Null input – leave the input blank	Not relevant

Surname is made up of alphanumeric characters so the most appropriate type is String.

Validation	Invalid data	Boundary data
Length check Any reasonable maximum length. Possibly 30 characters	Any data value of more than 30 characters	Data of 29, 30 and 31 characters
Presence check	Null input – leave the input blank	Not relevant

Chapter 10 Arrays

Reading from and Writing to an Array Extension Task

1 Appropriate validation approaches would include:

- range checks limiting the values of Index and IndexOut to the range 0 to 3

- type check limiting the values of DataItem to Integer values.

2 Figure 13.30(a) show the flowchart for the input validation, using decisions and looping to pass execution back to accepting input if invalid data is entered. Figure 13.30(b) shows the flowchart for the output validation. Figure 13.31 shows the corresponding pseudocode for the processes.

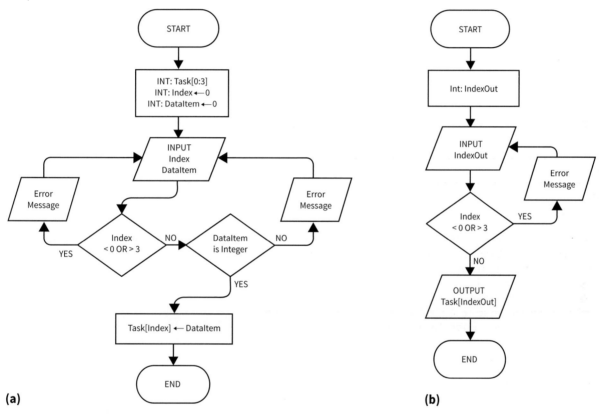

(a)   **(b)**

Figure 13.30 Flowcharts of possible Input and Output validation

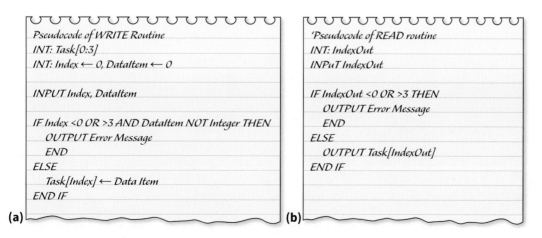

(a)   **(b)**

Figure 13.31 Pseudocode of possible Input and Output validation

The following code is an example of a Windows Forms Application:

```
Public Class Form1
    'Global declaration of the array to give scope to both subroutines
    Dim Task(3) As Integer

    Private Sub BTNInput_Click(sender As Object, e As EventArgs) Handles BTNInput.Click
        'Local declaration and initialisation of Input variables
        Dim Index As Integer = 0
        Dim DataItem As Integer = 0

        'Validation of user input
        'Validation split into two IF statements
        If TBIndex.Text < 0 Or TBIndex.Text > 3 Then
            MsgBox("Index must be between 0 and 3")
            Exit Sub
        Else
            Index = TBIndex.Text
        End If

        If Int32.TryParse(TBDataItem.Text, DataItem) = False Then
            MsgBox("Data Item must be an Integer")
            Exit Sub
        End If

        'Input of DataItem from user into selected index
        Task(Index) = DataItem
    End Sub

    Private Sub BTNOutput_Click(sender As Object, e As EventArgs) Handles BTNOutput.Click
        'Local declaration and initialisation of Output variable
        Dim IndexOut As Integer = 0

        'Validation of user selection of index to display
        If TBIndexOut.Text < 0 Or TBIndexOut.Text > 3 Then
            MsgBox("Index must be between 0 and 3")
            Exit Sub
        Else
            IndexOut = TBIndexOut.Text
        End If

        'Displaying the data item at selected index in the Textbox
        TBDisplay.Text = Task(IndexOut)
    End Sub
End Class
```

Iteration Extension Task

Figure 13.32 shows a flowchart and pseudocode for the algorithm.

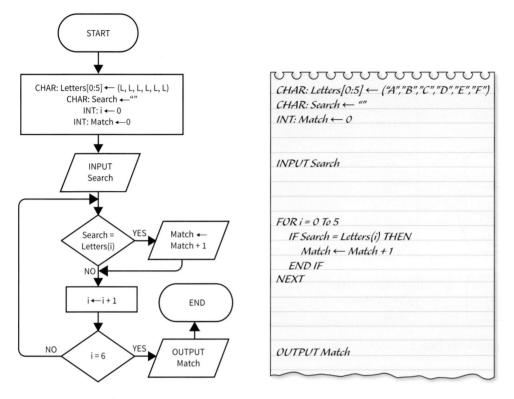

Figure 13.32 Flowchart and pseudocode for the iteration task

The following code is a possible solution:

```
'Subroutine to search the array
    Sub Search()
        Dim Search As Char = ""
        Dim Match As Integer = 0
        Console.WriteLine("Enter character for search")
        Search = Console.ReadLine

        For i = 0 To 5
            If Search = Letters(i) Then
                Match = Match + 1
            End If
        Next

        Console.WriteLine(Match)
        Console.ReadKey()

    End Sub
```

To test your code works change the characters held by the array to include repeated values. Inputting the repeated character as the search criteria should output the number of times the character is repeated in the array.

Array Task 1

Figure 13.33 shows a flowchart and pseudocode for the algorithm.

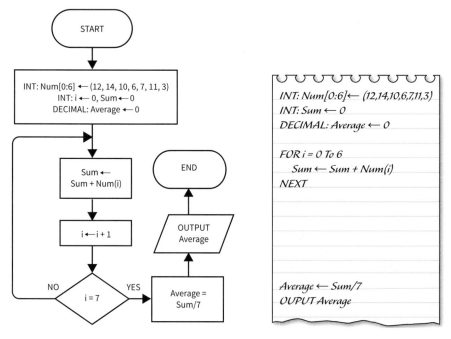

Figure 13.33 Flowchart and pseudocode for Task 1

The following code is a possible solution:

```
Module Module1
    Dim Num() As Integer = {12, 14, 10, 6, 7, 11, 3}

    Sub Main()

        Dim Sum As Integer = 0
        Dim Average As Decimal = 0

        For i = 0 To 6
            Sum = Sum + Num(i)
        Next

        Average = Sum / 7

        Console.WriteLine(Average)
        Console.ReadKey()

    End Sub

End Module
```

Array Task 2

Figure 13.34 shows a flowchart for the algorithms.

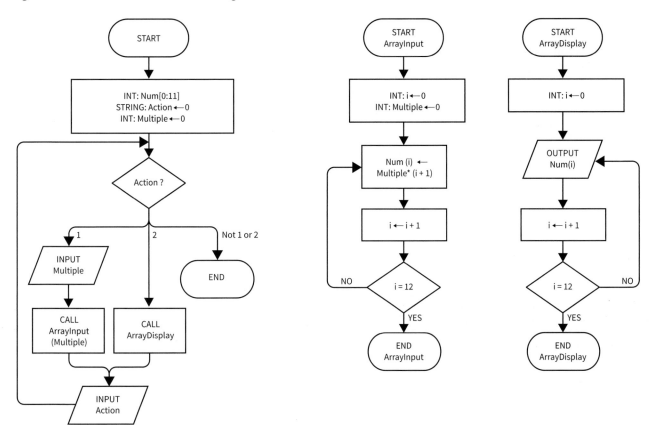

Figure 13.34 Flowchart for main program and required subroutines for Task 2

The following pseudocode shows a possible implementation:

```
'Pseudocode ArrayInput
SUB Input(INT: Multiple)
    FOR i = 0 To Length of Num – 1
        Num(i) ← Multiple * (i + 1)
    NEXT
END SUB


'Pseudocode for ArrayDisplay
SUB Display()
    FOR i = 0 To Length of Num – 1
        OUTPUT Num(i)
    NEXT
END SUB
```

```
'Pseudocode Main Subroutine
INT: Num[0:11]
INT: Action ← 1, Multiple ← 0
WHILE Action = 1 Or Action = 2 DO
    IF Action = 1 Then
        INPUT Multiple
        CALL Input(Multiple)
    ELSEIF Action = 2 THEN
        CALL Display
    END IF

    INPUT Action
LOOP
```

The following code is a possible Console Application solution:

```
Module Module1
    Dim Num(11) As Integer

    Sub Main()
        Dim Action As String = 1
        Dim Multiple As Integer = 0

        'Use of a While loop in the main subroutine to
        'control the user actions required
        Do While Action = 1 Or Action = 2
            'Use of IF..ELSE IF statement to provide appropriate
            'path dependant on user input
            If Action = 1 Then
                Console.WriteLine("Input a whole number")
                Multiple = Console.ReadLine
                'Call the subroutine and pass the required parameter
                Call ArrayInput(Multiple)
            ElseIf Action = 2 Then
                'Call the subroutine
                Call ArrayDisplay()
            End If
            'Once loop complete and control passed back to main routine
            'prompt the user for next action required.
            Console.WriteLine("To enter another number input 1")
            Console.WriteLine("To display multiples input 2")
            Console.WriteLine("To exit input any other number")
            Action = Console.ReadLine
        Loop
    End Sub

    'Subroutine to fill array with multiples
    'requires to be passed parameter when called
    Sub ArrayInput(Number As Integer)
        For i = 0 To 11
            'Note the (i + 1) to allow for the numbering from zero
            'without this the array would hold 0n to 11n
            Num(i) = Number * (i + 1)
        Next
    End Sub

    'Subroutine to display
    'Uses simple iteration and output command
    Sub ArrayDisplay()
        For i = 0 To 11
            Console.WriteLine(Num(i))
        Next
    End Sub
End Module
```

Array Task 3

Figure 13.35 shows a flowchart and pseudocode for the algorithm.

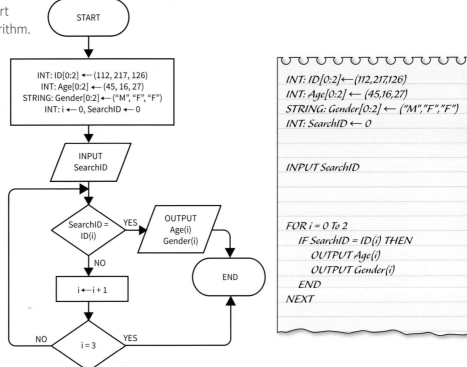

Figure 13.35 Flowchart for Task 3

The following code is a possible solution:

```
Module Module1
    'Group of arrays to hold related data items
    Dim ID() As Integer = {112, 217, 126}
    Dim Age() As Integer = {45, 16, 27}
    Dim Gender() As String = {"M", "F", "F"}
    Sub Main()
        'Declare and obtain user search input
        Dim SearchID As Integer = 0
        Console.WriteLine("Insert ID to Search")
        SearchID = Console.ReadLine

        'Use FOR loop to loop through all index positions
        For i = 0 To 2
            'Check SearchID against all positions in ID array
            'if a match is found then display the data from the
            'other arrays at the same index position that match found
            If SearchID = ID(i) Then
                Console.WriteLine(Age(i))
                Console.WriteLine(Gender(i))
                Console.ReadKey()
                Exit Sub
            End If
        Next

        'Output message if no match found
        'Had a match been located the Exit Sub would have
        'terminated execution before this line is read
        Console.WriteLine("No Match with ID")
        Console.ReadKey()
    End Sub
End Module
```

Chapter 11 Directional Instructions

Iteration Task

1 It is possible to make use of repetition in a number of areas. Instructions 4 to 7 repeat the sequence FORWARD 90, RIGHT 90 twice. Instructions also repeat at either instruction 12 to 15 or instruction 13 to 16.

2 It would be possible to rewrite the instructions using a REPEAT..ENDREPEAT sequence:

Instruction number	Instruction
4	REPEAT 2
5	FORWARD 40
6	RIGHT 90
7	ENDREPEAT

The repetition instructions cause the turtle to complete the actions within the REPEAT.. ENDREPEAT loop twice. Remember that when using REPEAT commands it is crucial to indicate:

- the number of times the sequence of instructions must be completed

- where to end the repeated sequence.

Floor Turtle Task 1

Without use of REPEAT:

1 LEFT 90
2 PENDOWN
3 FORWARD 50
4 RIGHT 90
5 FORWARD 70
6 RIGHT 90
7 FORWARD 20
8 RIGHT 90
9 FORWARD 20
10 LEFT 90
11 FORWARD 20
12 LEFT 90
13 FORWARD 20
14 RIGHT 90
15 FORWARD 20
16 RIGHT 90
17 FORWARD 20
18 LEFT 90
19 FORWARD 20
20 LEFT 90
21 FORWARD 20
22 RIGHT 90
23 FORWARD 20
24 RIGHT 90
25 FORWARD 70
26 RIGHT 90
27 FORWARD 20

REPEAT Option 1:

1 LEFT 90
2 PENDOWN
3 FORWARD 50
4 RIGHT 90
5 FORWARD 70
6 REPEAT 2
7   RIGHT 90
8   FORWARD 20
9 ENDREPEAT
10 REPEAT 2
11   LEFT 90
12   FORWARD 20
13 ENDREPEAT
14 REPEAT 2
15   RIGHT 90
16   FORWARD 20
17 ENDREPEAT
18 REPEAT 2
19   LEFT 90
20   FORWARD 20
21 ENDREPEAT
22 RIGHT 90
23 FORWARD 20
24 RIGHT 90
25 FORWARD 70
26 RIGHT 90
27 FORWARD 20

REPEAT Option 2:

1 LEFT 90
2 PENDOWN
3 FORWARD 50
4 RIGHT 90
5 FORWARD 70
6 REPEAT 2
7   RIGHT 90
8   FORWARD 20
9   RIGHT 90
10   FORWARD 20
11   LEFT 90
12   FORWARD 20
13   LEFT 90
14   FORWARD 20
15 ENDREPEAT
16 RIGHT 90
17 FORWARD 20
18 RIGHT 90
19 FORWARD 70
20 RIGHT 90
21 FORWARD 20

Floor Turtle Task 2

1 LEFT 90	**10** RIGHT 45	**19** FORWARD 120
2 PENDOWN	**11** FORWARD 20	**20** RIGHT 90
3 FORWARD 20	**12** PENUP	**21** FORWARD 20
4 RIGHT 45	**13** FORWARD 40	**22** RIGHT 45
5 FORWARD 56	**14** PENDOWN	**23** FORWARD 28
6 RIGHT 45	**15** FORWARD 40	**24** LEFT 90
7 FORWARD 60	**16** RIGHT 45	**25** FORWARD 28
8 RIGHT 45	**17** FORWARD 28	**26** RIGHT 90
9 FORWARD 56	**18** RIGHT 45	**27** FORWARD 28

Floor Turtle Task 3

1 LEFT 90	**6** ENDREPEAT	**11** FORWARD 28
2 PENDOWN	**7** FORWARD 20	**12** PENDOWN
3 REPEAT 3	**8** RIGHT 45	**13** FORWARD 28
4 FORWARD 120	**9** FORWARD 56	**14** LEFT 135
5 RIGHT 90	**10** PENUP	**15** FORWARD 60

Chapter 12 Examination Practice

Mark scheme for exam-style questions

1

Size	Country	Output	
20	USA	10	(1 mark)
19	France	19	(1 mark)
14	UK	16	(1 mark)

2

Error	Effect	Correction	
Small has been initialised to zero	Small is likely to be smaller than any of the array values and will not be changed by the comparison with the number input.	Either of following would be acceptable: Initialise Small with a large number. OR Assign the value of NUM(1) to Small before any comparison is made with the remaining array values.	(1 mark for error) (1 mark for correction)
`Num(Counter) ←` `Small`	The value of Small is placed into the array.	`Small ← Num(Counter)`	(1 mark for error) (1 mark for correction)
The loop counter is incremented twice	Next automatically increments the loop but the following line also increments the loop counter: `Counter ← Counter + 1` Consequently only the odd number indexes will be read.	Remove the line `Counter ← Counter + 1`	(1 mark for error) (1 mark for correction)
Small is output from within the FOR loop	The system will output the current value of Small on every iteration.	Put the OUTPUT line after NEXT.	(1 mark for error) (1 mark for correction)

3

Time	Total	Number	Count	Average	Output
0	0	0	0		
18	18	0	1		
19	37	0	2		
24	61	1	3		
21	82	2	4		
18	100	2	5		
17	117	2	6		
23	140	3	7		
20	160	4	8		
19	179	4	9		
21	200	5	10		
−1	200	5	10	20	
					20, 5
(1 mark)	(1 mark)	(1 mark)	(1 mark)	(1 mark)	(1 mark)

It is likely that mistakes would not be penalised twice. As a result if the Total, Number or Count are incorrect the marks will be lost in those columns. However if those incorrect values have been used to produce the Average and Output then the marks for those columns may well remain.

The Time, Total, Number, Count columns must start with a zero – the algorithm initialised the variables and this should be included in the trace table. The Average and Output columns must not contain values (not even zero) during the execution of the loop. They are outside the loop in the algorithm and do not take a value before the input of the final −1.

4   Any effective algorithm will gain marks; this is an example:

```
INPUT N1, N2, N3
IF N1 < N2 AND N1 < N3 THEN
    OUTPUT N1
ELSE
    IF N2 < N3 THEN
        OUTPUT N2
    ELSE
        OUTPUT N3
    END IF
END IF
```

Correct method to find smallest where N1 is smallest.   (1 mark)

Correct method to find smallest where N2 is smallest.   (1 mark)

Correct method to find smallest where N3 is smallest.   (1 mark)

5

Data input	Validation technique	Invalid test data
Mobile phone number	**Length check:** 10 or 11 characters	Any invalid data, e.g. 07716 123 or 07736 123456789
	Format check: NNNNN–NNNNNN	ABCDE_123456
Height	**Type check:** Real (not Integer; Height is continuous data will not be only whole numbers)	Any invalid data, e.g. 2½ or "Ninety centimetres"
	Range check: 0.25 to 3 meters (accept other sensible ranges)	4.6 metres, 1 cm
Number of brothers	**Type check:** Integer (must be a whole number, so not Real or Short)	4.3, Four
	Range check: 0 to 20 (any sensible large value)	–2, not zero – you can have no brothers

For each of the data items:

Correct validation method   (1 mark)

Appropriate test data – must match the validation method stated   (1 mark)

                                                         Total of 6 marks

6

Number	Count	Output
11	0	
8	1	
5	2	
2	3	
–1	4	4
9	0	
6	1	
3	2	
0	3	
–3	4	4
–2		End of sequence

1 mark for each correct section as indicated above.

Output must not contain any additional items

             Total of 4 marks

7

```
PENDOWN
RIGHT 90
REPEAT 3
```

```
FORWARD    30
RIGHT      90
ENDREPEAT
```

```
FORWARD    10
LEFT       90
FORWARD    30
PEN UP
```

```
FORWARD    10
PEN DOWN
FORWARD    10
RIGHT      90
```

```
FORWARD    20
RIGHT      90
FORWARD    30
```

Accept any correct solution e.g. LEFT 270 for RIGHT 90

Ignore any instructions used to reset the turtle after reaching the Finish.

1 mark for each correct section indicated   Total of 4 marks

8 1 mark for each correctly completed section indicated

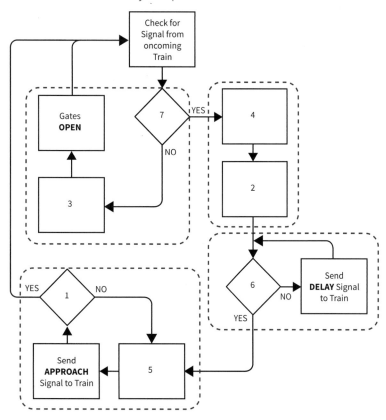

9 Any effective algorithm will gain marks; this is an example:

```
INPUT TargetScore
FOR Counter = 1 To 6
    IF SCORE(Counter) > TargetScore THEN
        OUTPUT NAME(Counter)
        OUTPUT ID(Counter)
    END IF
NEXT
```

Correct loop to iterate six times	(1 mark)
Correct comparison for TargetScore	(1 mark)
Correct output of NAME and ID within loop	(1 mark)

10 Any effective algorithm will gain marks; these are examples:

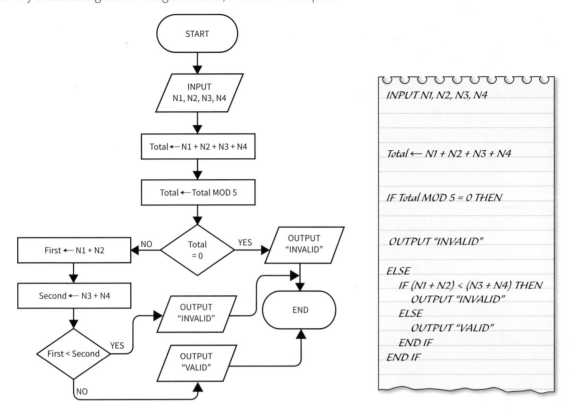

No need to use Total, First and Second as shown in example. Could be achieved in a single step.

Correct calculation of Total	(1 mark)
Correct check that not a multiple of 5	(1 mark)
Correct calculation of First and Second	(1 mark)
Correct comparison of First and Second	(1 mark)
Correct output of "INVALID" from both paths	(1 mark)
Correct output of "VALID"	(1 mark)
	Total of 6 marks